CHASING
GOD

CHASING GOD

ONE MAN'S MIRACULOUS JOURNEY
IN THE HEART OF THE CITY

ROGER HUANG

and Susanna Foth Aughtmon

transforming lives together

CHASING GOD
Published by David C Cook
4050 Lee Vance View
Colorado Springs, CO 80918 U.S.A.

David C Cook Distribution Canada
55 Woodslee Avenue, Paris, Ontario, Canada N3L 3E5

David C Cook U.K., Kingsway Communications
Eastbourne, East Sussex BN23 6NT, England

The graphic circle C logo is a registered trademark of David C Cook.

LCCN 2013939005
ISBN 978-1-4347-0595-2
eISBN 978-1-4347-0716-1

© 2013 Roger Huang
Published in association with the Books & Such Literary Agency, 52 Mission Circle,
Suite 122, PMB 170, Santa Rosa, CA 95409-5370, www.booksandsuch.com.

The Team: Don Pape, John Blase, Amy Konyndyk,
Nick Lee, Tonya Osterhouse, Karen Athen
Cover Design: Nick Lee
Cover Photo: Shutterstock

Printed in the United States of America

First Edition 2013

1 2 3 4 5 6 7 8 9 10

062813

CONTENTS

ACKNOWLEDGMENTS

I would like to thank each person who has helped me and loved me through this journey of chasing God. First and foremost, I want to thank my children and their spouses who have given their lives to this work and who are passionate about Jesus. I love you with all my heart!

Marie France, you are wise, godly, beautiful, and passionate.

Philip, you are independent, a hard worker, and a great provider for your family.

Michelle, you are beautiful, stubborn, and caring. You always look out for me.

Christian, you love God and people. You have so much grace. You're the one who makes us laugh! You are a peacemaker.

For my grandchildren, Clayton, Cade, Cal, Elle Louise, Kahaleana, Gabrielle, Abraham, Ezra, Isabelle, Sophie, Canaan, Joelle, Malachi, Micah, Maiya, and Hunter. I love each of you so much! You are the reason I want to stay close to home. I want to be with you every moment of my life. May God use you in a great way. May His mercy and grace be upon you.

Clint, you are dedicated, faithful, and a hard worker. You are a lover of souls.

Rossie, you're filled with grace. You are godly and beautiful. You show me grace.

Cori, you are my personal counselor. You're godly and beautiful.

Jody, you are so kind and patient. You are a great listener!

I love you all and am thankful for each of you every day. My heart overflows with thanksgiving at God's mercy over my family.

To each person who has invested his or her time and resources and passion into our mission here in the Tenderloin, I cannot thank you enough. This list should go into the thousands. I am thankful for each person who has poured himself or herself out, loving the poor, giving of their time and energy to show Jesus to those here in the Tenderloin. I would like to give a special thanks to each person who has worked and volunteered at City Academy, the rescue mission, the thrift store, and for our countless community outreaches. If your name is not mentioned, just know that we would not be here without you and we love you!

Ed and Sandi Morgan, thank you for the opportunity to serve in your church when I first got saved.

Lula Baird, you prayed with us and invited us into the Assemblies of God. You were the reason they took us in. Thank you so much for your passion and love for God's work in the Tenderloin. I miss you so much.

Terry and Vicky Wong, you were my first helpers in the Tenderloin. Thank you for your love and support!

May Chan, thank you for praying for over twenty years for God to send someone to the Tenderloin. We are the answer to your prayers!

Mary Cheng, Connie, and Angela, thank you for leading the ESL classes with the immigrants. You were my inspiration!

Mrs. Chan and Susan Lee, thank you for your help every Saturday making sandwiches and feeding the kids. Susan Lee, thank you for your faithfulness and continuous support for twenty-nine years.

Mr. and Mrs. Sun, for giving me the bag of gold coins to help me purchase the building. Thank you!

Donald Annas, thank you for accepting me into your fellowship. You were like a father to me.

James Braddy, you encouraged me to keep going when I didn't know what to do. Thank you!

Glen Cole, you trusted me and gave me your endorsement. You were my mentor. I miss you!

Jack and Chris Schat, you provided a place of refuge where I could rest my heart and spirit with your beautiful home by the coast. That is priceless. You spoke to me with your smiles and kindness.

Dean Heath, you rallied your church and gave us a working commercial kitchen.

Karl Stewart, you helped me when there was no one else to turn to. You gave me financial help time after time through your church. I appreciate your help and your trust in this work.

Kevin and Gayla Compton, you single-handedly helped me time after time when there was no other way out for me. You gave without reservation. God bless you.

Mel Keys, you never stopped talking about God's goodness and faithfulness! You kept me going!

Dennis and Deanna Smith, your love, support, and encouragement have lifted me many times.

Rick Cole, thank you for your friendship and continued support.

Mike and Wendy Nelson, you gave and served with us year after year.

Mark Heath, thank you for your friendship and support. You taught me grace—and kindness!

Ben Hardister, you are a mover, a maverick, and a giver. You are daring and courageous. You helped us for two years when there was no one else in sight.

Karen Hardister, you're an immovable presence, and I thank you for interceding for us.

Scott and Barb Farmer, you rallied behind your church and gave us a new building. You gave your resources to an inner-city work you knew nothing about. Your love for the poor and the children in the Tenderloin community is evident. I am overwhelmed by your passion.

Dick Sanner, you have shown grace in leading the team from your church and working with Fred and Jan to complete our building project. You are a man of compassion and grace. You became a mentor by visiting me often and sharing your dream about wanting to do more for the rest of the world.

Marsha King, thank you for your continued intercession and for being the one God used to bring many to help the mission.

Jeff and Beth Farrington, you two were a power team, always helping the children and the poor. I miss Beth so much! Jeff, you're a true servant and ambassador!

Connie Crank, thank you for serving and for your passion.

Mike and Laura McMillen, you gave me the hope and courage to continue. You are my friends and advisors.

Craig and Rheanell Farrill, thank you for loving God's people and investing in this work.

Fred and Jan Hull, you built us a school building. You led over four thousand volunteers in doing so, and you were an answer to prayer. You are like John the Baptist. You lifted our spirits and our confidence. You gave us a head start. It was a once-in-a-lifetime miracle. I still cannot believe you gave us a brand-new building with the space for 350 students. I am in awe of your love, sacrifice, and obedience. God bless you both and your loved ones!

Scott and Kelli Welchek, you have been so generous, caring, and loving. I love being around you!

Tom and Josie Dowd, when I thought you were pushing me, you were actually pulling me. Your love and motivation kept me going! Your constant advice and your investment in me give me confidence. Love you much.

Howard and Judy Guild, thank you for your love and investment in our inner-city elementary school. Your love for the children and the teachers is a great encouragement. Thank you.

Bob and Linda Currie, thank you for inviting the entire school to your home and for continuing to support us with your resources.

Jim and Celeste Ornellas, you invited us to your magnificent home and introduced your friends to this work without reservation. You gave me permission to call you whenever I was in need of help. I am in awe of your generosity and friendship.

Brad Franklin, you gave your church the freedom to get involved with this work. You have blessed us time and time again. I am grateful for your passionate heart and commitment to the poor.

John and Mary Ann Ray, you brought over one thousand volunteers to the Tenderloin community and continue to bless us every month with birthday celebrations for the children in our school. Your love for the children brings joy and excitement to these little ones. Thank you for driving such a long distance just to be with the children.

Jim Haden, you are a man of order and you're a big help to this work.

Doug Thompson, thank you for serving the mission with passion.

David and Eli Gardner, you were the first to give me a chance to share at the Entertainment Art headquarters. You brought your good friends from Menlo Park and Atherton to give us a second chance.

Ted and Sara Lucas, you gave your support to keep our school going. You worked tirelessly even when you were busy building your own business. Your smiles and passion, and the hours of sharing this work with your friends, have given us so much hope and joy. God bless you for loving the children.

John and Nancy Ortberg, thank you for believing in this work. You have commissioned your church to help us with over fifteen hundred people in the past three years. Your leadership is filled with passion and has stirred the fire in many hearts.

Chuck and Leslie King, you showed me God's grace and you are so selfless. You have not stopped pouring into this work. Thank you for having us over to your beautiful home time after time. God bless you and your loved ones.

Bill and Kristin Eberwein, what a great team you are! You are warriors, passionate worshippers, and encouragers. You have blessed me! May God shower you and bless you beyond your imagination.

Thank you, Kristin and Leslie, for believing in me!

Kevin Kim, thank you for loving us. You are a man of compassion.

Veasna and Elaine Chea, you have served tirelessly and prayed continuously for so long. You are like my own kids. I love you both!

Laura Soun, your smile and your love for the children bring me so much joy. I love you so much.

Ralph Gella, thank you for your faithfulness and hard work! God bless you!

Carlos Jackson, you're a faithful and hard worker, and I thank you!

Terry and Kathleen Lu, your passion for souls gives me strength to continue. You inspire me! Your passion for God's work is inspiring.

Mark Holmstedt, your wisdom and love for this work are priceless.

Sue Aughtmon, thank you for writing this book for me. I couldn't have done it without you! You gave me completeness in sharing with you. You are more than a writer. You are a great listener. You have blessed me in more ways than one.

Francis and Lisa Chan, you came to serve without reservation. You reached out to the poor with your hearts. Your family is a blessing to this work. God bless you in your calling.

David Acker, you came with one agenda—to reach the poor and love them unconditionally. You are amazing.

Wendy Lawton, Don Pape, John Blase, and the entire team at David C Cook, you believed in me and gave me a chance to share my story so that others may have a chance to experience God in the most personal way. Thank you for doing what you do. God bless you.

To my wife, Maite, you have restored me with your love, patience, and hours of travailing for my brokenness. You taught me how to love and enjoy life. You taught me what commitment is. You gave me a chance to live again. Your laughter, patience, and godliness have given me so much hope and joy. It's been thirty-seven years, but it feels like we've just met. You're an excellent wife, mother, grandmother, and my best friend. I am glad I was persistent in chasing you!

Finally, I would like to thank You, God, for giving me a chance to experience Your great power, love, and grace. I cannot believe that You love me that much. You gave me more than I could imagine and ask for and I can only thank You in words. Thank You for giving me eternal life through Your Son, Jesus.

FOREWORD

BY JOHN ORTBERG

For about two thousand years or so, Jesus has been showing up in the most unlikely places. It started in a manger. Then in a dirty little river where He decided to get baptized. You never know where He might pop us next: in the home of a tax collector or the presence of a despised adulteress or in a conversation with a Gentile; in a deserted garden or at a sham trial or on a cruel cross.

He gave a warning about these appearances once. He talked about marginalized people: the forgotten, the impoverished, the imprisoned, the destitute. "Whatever you do to the least of these," He said, "you do to Me."

No leader of a religion had ever talked like this before. No one had talked like this period. And ever since then, people have been finding Jesus in and following Him into the strangest places. Like Waldo, you can look at the page for a long time before you locate the Man from Nazareth.

Roger is one of those who has been following and finding Jesus. San Francisco can be a glamorous place, but also hard and lonely and cruel. It takes practice to see Jesus there. And Roger has been practicing a long while.

In this book, he tells his story with candor and openness, courage and grace. He speaks of his own past and his own pain; of the way the grace of God was opened up to him in a fashion he could not have predicted. But through his entire journey, God was at work to prepare a man who could also help others find Jesus and who could find Jesus in others. Roger has had a journey of extraordinary faith, where God called him to do that which was far beyond himself, and he said yes, and God acted.

Kind of like in the early church. When someone says yes, a divine energy is at work that can never be explained in human terms.

A friend of mine reminded me that spending time with Roger—kind of like spending time with Jesus—is always dangerous. People start making changes in their lives, finding ways to free up Tuesday to come down and tutor or prepare meals or work in a library or knock on doors to deliver groceries, to come home tired and stretched and amazed to find out they had actually been on the adventure Jesus had invited them to long ago.

Perhaps it's been a while since you've had an adventure.

In that case, I'm glad you'll get to meet Roger. Once you know something of his story, it'll be time to launch out on a new chapter of your own.

Chapter 1

BREAKDOWN

San Francisco, 1983
He spoke to me. It was clear and graphic.

Breaking down in San Francisco's Tenderloin district is not the best way to start the day. But this is the place that God has chosen to speak to me.

Of course, I don't know this as I make my way up the trash-littered sidewalk toward my car. No one in their right mind would go to the Tenderloin to hear God speak. And if my car's flat tire is any indication, it seems like God isn't taking much notice of me at the moment. A broken-down car is the last thing I need. Rubbing my forehead with a tired hand, I look around, taking in my shady surroundings. The Tenderloin is San Francisco at its seediest, where bad things happen and corruption wreaks havoc. A place where you hold your breath and your wallet and try to get out as fast as you can. I'm not thinking about God or listening for His voice as I kneel down to look at my tire. I just want to go home. The rim is almost touching the ground. I let out a huge sigh and glance around for a pay phone.

Looking up Turk Street, I see a crowded city block full of dirty, worn-out buildings. Broken bottles pool around an overflowing trash can. A trickle of homeless people shuffles down the sidewalk. Small pockets of thrill seekers mill around the doors of a bathhouse. A drug dealer, baseball cap pulled down low on his head, bends toward the window of a blue car near the intersection. I spot a phone booth by a run-down liquor store as I head up the street toward Parc 55, the hotel I work at.

Making a wide circle, I step around a strung-out young man propped up in the doorway of an empty storefront. Greasy locks of hair peek out from under his knit cap. He clutches a ratty blanket around his shoulders.

The unpleasant smell of rotting produce assaults me as an older lady with yellowing and gray hair and a baggy pink dress sidles up to me. "You got something for me?"

"Sorry. Not today." I shake my head and brush past her. *Get me out of here.* I glance back over my shoulder toward Union Square. Maybe I should have just gone back to the office. It smells a lot better there.

San Francisco is a patchwork of rich and poor districts. High- and low-class neighborhoods butt up against each other. The fact that the posh hotel where I work is a few blocks from one of the poorest neighborhoods in the city just makes it easier to find affordable parking.

Knowing what I know now, I should have paid to park in a garage. But this is one of my first days on the job as an auditor for Parc 55.

The hotel is a dream. All plush furniture and chandeliers and class. Like the people who stay there. Newly opened, the opulent hotel was built by a rich, young Asian businessman. His dream hotel takes up an entire city block.

I thumb through the phone book and find a nearby towing company. Waiting for the company to pick up, I think back to the day I had interviewed at Parc 55.

Straight off the night shift at the Crowne Plaza in Burlingame, I'd rushed home to shower and put on a fresh shirt. Maite (pronounced *My-tay*) was in the kitchen pouring milk into her steaming cup of coffee. The older kids, Marie France and Phil, were already at school. The little ones, Michelle and Christian, were still asleep.

"Where are you going?"

Looping my tie around my neck, I paused to kiss my wife. "I'm going down to Parc 55 to interview."

Her eyebrows lifted in surprise. "Roger, people slept all night in line out there. Don't bother going."

I threaded the tie end through the knot. I knew what I was doing. I could feel the excitement building in my chest. This was the type of hotel where I wanted to work. I liked large hotels with lots of rooms and lots of class. The bigger the better, and this one was the newest crown jewel of downtown San Francisco. It was my dream job.

"It's all right. I'm going to check it out."

She smiled. "You have two auditing jobs already. Do you really need another one?"

Brushing back a wayward strand of her dark, curly hair, I pecked her on the cheek and grabbed my suit coat. "Don't worry about it."

I closed the apartment door behind me and jogged out to my car. The city was coming alive in the early morning hours. Storefronts were rolling back their gates and unlocking their doors. Commuters headed into car parks and pushed through the doors of their glass-fronted office buildings. The usual symphony of car horns and muted sirens filtered through the wispy, fog-filled air. I threaded my way through the traffic congestion that was hedging its way around Union Square and parked only to find the entire block was cordoned off. There were a lot of other folks who wanted jobs at Parc 55. The line stretched down past the hotel, snaking its way around the corner.

I drew in a deep breath. *This was going to be a long wait. A long wait.* As I headed past the gleaming front door of Parc 55 toward the back of the line, I made eye contact with the doorman. To my surprise, he nodded and smiled, opening the door for me.

"Thank you," I said, as I stepped inside.

"Yes, sir." He smiled at me again.

Maybe he thinks I am the son of the Chinese millionaire who just built this hotel. Maybe that's why he let me in. I'm not telling him any different.

I grinned to myself, thankful for my good luck, and looked around. The lobby was wide and lit with sunlight. A murmur of friendly voices filled the room. Men in sharp business suits were seated on luxurious sofas and sleek chairs. A large crystal chandelier sent a soft, filtered light cascading down. People at the front desk readied papers and chatted brightly. This was going to be big. Huge. A brand-new modern hotel in the heart of Union Square. I wanted in. Not wanting the doorman's mistake to be found out, I slipped through the lobby to the restrooms. I waited there until I heard them start calling names for interviews.

Three days later I had the job.

Three weeks later, I'm here, stuck with a flat in the Tenderloin. There's nothing classy or plush about that.

With a click, the ringing stops and a lady with a nasal voice picks up. The tow truck will be here in twenty minutes. I make my way back down the street.

A barker hawking a strip show steps in my path. Nodding toward the blinking neon sign he is standing under, he tells me, "We've got a lot of pretty girls.... It's a good time."

"No, thanks." I push past him.

"You're missing out!" he yells after me.

I kick a stray beer can in my path toward the curb.

A group of teenage gangsters clustered near the stoplight on the corner jostle each other and call out, "Hey, baby! Why don't you come over here?" I follow their shouts and line of sight to a young woman in a too-short miniskirt on the opposite corner. All I want is to get home to my couch to take a nap.

I pop open the door of my car and slide into the front seat. Shaking open my newspaper, I try to take in the headlines. News. Politics. Sports. The 49ers are on top of the world. You can't walk anywhere in the city without hearing the names Montana and Lott spoken in reverent tones. This city bleeds red and gold.

I suck in a deep breath and roll my shoulders. *Breathe. Just breathe.*

I settle in for the wait. Out of the corner of my eye, I notice a commotion on the sidewalk. The cluster of teenagers on the corner have moved their attention to a younger boy who is standing next to the front door of a run-down high-rise. Surrounding him, they circle like predators. His head is bowed with fear, and his narrow shoulders are hunched forward. I hear their muffled words through my window.

"What do you got in here? Can I have some?" A skinny boy with long black hair grabs at the boy's pockets, pulling at his frayed pants.

A round-faced teen with a red denim jacket pins the kid against the wall as the others take turns swatting at his face. "Let me go! Let me go!" he cries.

Immediately, my hands go slick with sweat and a wave of nausea sweeps over me. I touch a dry tongue to my lips. Violence always has this effect on me. It is not foreign to me. I grew up in a country where cruelty and bribery were the daily currency. I hate violence with every part of my being.

I watch as the boy bends beneath their rough hands. A sense of revulsion roils in my stomach as the teenagers' laughter and curses puncture the air.

I tear my eyes away, focusing on the paper. I can sense the hopelessness in that boy as if I am pressed against the wall next to him, as if I am feeling the blows and the fear that cramps his body.

Where are the police anyway? What kind of neighborhood leaves its children out on the streets alone to fend off drug dealers and cruel bullies?

I feel sick seeing someone get hurt, but I know enough about this neighborhood to not get involved.

A knock on the window startles me. "Are you the one with the flat?"

The face of the mechanic fills my window. I roll it down. "Yes! Thank you so much for coming."

Within minutes, I am headed home. Smooth, tall skyscrapers and corner grocery stores replace rickety buildings and barred tenements as I follow the streets back to our apartment. The afternoon sun warms the inside of the car, releasing the scent of newsprint and air freshener.

I push Fleetwood Mac into the tape player, attempting to calm my uneven breathing and the pulsing headache that is coming on. Music is my escape. I turn it up in an attempt to rid myself of the images that are flooding my mind. The words and melody fill the car, chasing away the hopelessness that crowded my mind a few seconds earlier. At least it does for a moment.

Somehow that scene, that boy with his sad eyes and his face full of fear, keeps coming back to me. Pictures of him flash like snapshots through my head. His hands in front of his face. His jacket twisting around him as he tries to break free from their grasp. His frail body pressing up against the grubby building.

I rub my forehead with a shaking hand and try to turn my thoughts toward my wife, Maite, and the kids. Her infectious laugh. Their smiling faces. The small pieces of joy they weave into my life each day. In these moments of trying to forget, it happens. A single riveting thought clears every image from my mind: *What would you have done if that were your son?* The thought is as clear as if someone were sitting in the passenger seat next to me, speaking to me.

My gut clenches in a visceral reaction as I imagine Phil and Christian at the mercy of a bunch of thugs. *No one lays a hand on either of my sons. I would have helped him. Protected him.*

In a bright moment of clarity, the next thought pierces me with a swift and sharp conviction: *They are all the same to Me.*

I have never heard God speak to me before, but I know His voice in the way a child recognizes his father's. He is sharing His heart with me … and it is broken.

I can barely see well enough to make it home. Tears blur my vision, and I draw in a ragged breath as I open the door to the apartment. Maite is standing by the kitchen sink preparing dinner. One glance at me, and she puts the vegetables she is chopping to the side.

"Roger, what's wrong?" She knows the ins and outs of me and my moods.

I walk over and grip her in a fierce hug, holding her tight. The scent of her, the warmth of her arms, unleashes a torrent of sorrow that has lived in me for so long, I can't contain my tears. Head cradled against her shoulder, I can't utter a word. The cotton of her shirt is soaked as I cry against her neck.

"What happened to you? Are you okay?"

I am sobbing—deep, gut-wrenching sobs. The Holy Spirit is at work, shifting things in my spirit, touching me, speaking to me in a way that He never has before. Loosening my hold on Maite, I turn to the sofa.

"Roger, you have to talk to me. Tell me what happened." She follows me to the sofa.

Pressing my knees to the floor, I kneel by the sofa. Tears of regret and sadness just keep coming.

She sits on the sofa, a warm hand resting on my head. "Please talk to me, Roger, so I can help you."

Lifting my head to look at her, I press the heels of my palms into my swollen eyes and try to speak. My breathing is labored and cut with sadness. The story comes in fits and starts. Slowly I tell her about my morning and the scene unfolds. I watch as Maite's face mirrors my own pain. Tears slip from the corners of her eyes as she pieces the story together. The bullies, their cruelty, and the fear of the little boy.

"Roger, what happened to the boy? Is he okay?" Her forehead crinkles with concern.

"I don't know," I whisper. "I didn't help him. I left." I see disappointment cloud her eyes. "And then on the way home, this thought, this voice asked me, 'What would you have done if that was your son?' and I said I would have helped him...." A sob rips through my body.

"What, Roger?"

Lifting my eyes to meet hers again, I say, "I said I would have helped him. And then the voice said, 'They are all the same to Me.' They are all the same to Me. It was God, Maite. God spoke to me."

I have been praying for months, years even, asking God to speak to me in a real and clear way. I can't believe that this is the moment He has chosen to speak, and it's because I've broken His heart. At this thought, every last bit of composure drains from me, and I collapse, full-length, on the carpet.

Maite sits next to me. I know she is crying with me. Body heaving, I weep as I have not wept for years. Not even when I was fired a few years earlier and had hidden in the bathroom to cry so Maite and the kids wouldn't hear me. This is different. There is no fear, just a building ache inside of me for the boy who was hurt and for all the children who had ever felt the pain of abuse and neglect. My pain cannot be formed with words.

Years later, I would know this as the pivotal moment where God began to reshape my thinking and my life, changing me from the inside out. But in this moment, I can only think that I have failed God, that little boy, and myself.

That boy, that poor boy, with his hands covering his face and fear bending his body, is God's boy. His child. No different to God than Philip or Christian are to me. And I turned away from him. I read my newspaper and drove away, leaving him to his misery. I groan. A fresh wave of grief rolls over me.

The carpet is damp beneath my face. I cry, knowing I have forgotten that God loves the least of these and that I have let Him down. I cry, realizing that I am not the man I want to be. I cry for the little boy I left hurting in the Tenderloin. I cry, because I hadn't run to his rescue and saved him from his attackers.

And I cry for another little boy I once knew. A frightened little boy who knew the pain of blow after vicious blow, who knew the sharpness of cruelty and the sorrow of never being rescued. I cry for myself.

Pressing my hands to the sides of my head, trying to will the inevitable to stop, a thousand dreaded memories wash over me, and I am back in the corner of a darkened room in Taipei.

Chapter 2

LOST AND ALONE

Taipei, 1966
How do you mend a broken heart?

The room is muggy with the damp air of a summer night. A cricket sings on a tree somewhere. A yellow slit of light from the hallway squeezes under the door. I close my eyes tight—so tight that I cannot see the light. *If I close my eyes tight enough, maybe I can be somewhere else. Be someone else.* My palms ache and pain shoots up my knees into my hips. My arms and shoulders sting from the reddening welts that mark them. I am on all fours, naked, in the dark of my room. I can hear my brothers breathing heavily in the dark next to me. They are older than I am. They can kneel longer than I can. My legs usually start to shake after the first hour.

Our two younger brothers and sister are asleep down the hall, oblivious to our midnight torment. There are six of us children total, but only we three older boys bear the brunt of our father's anger. We don't know why. It is just the way it is.

One of my older brothers snickers. "I hope he fell down and knocked himself out."

"Shhhh! He'll hear you!"

"I don't care."

I feel the tears gathering against my eyelids, pressing their way through my lashes. "Please," I whisper, "be quiet. Don't make him come in again." I am desperate for them to be quiet, trying to hold back the inevitable. I don't know why we are being punished, but I know if I just wait, it will be over soon. I have trained myself to wait for the end.

When we make him angry enough, the beatings can stretch into one seemingly endless, terrifying night.

The door is flung open, and the blinding light from the hall frames our father's silhouette in the doorway. He is a giant. A monster. We can't see his face, but we have memorized its angry lines and cruel contours.

"So you don't believe me when I tell you not to talk? I will make you believe me. Don't talk!" His calm voice builds into a scream. He lunges for my oldest brother with a hard round stick, beating the backs of his legs and his shoulders. My dad takes pleasure in tormenting us in different ways. My brother refuses to make a sound. He takes the beating as if he deserves it. He grunts as he is lifted from the ground by the force of my father's kick. As my brother rolls over, my dad punches him in the stomach. My fear feeds the hard knot of hatred growing in the pit of my stomach. I see my brother curling into a ball, trying to protect his face.

"Get up! Get up, you worthless idiot!" My other brother tries to scoot away from my father to escape the backlash. His movement catches my father's eye. He is next.

Dropping the stick, my father grabs him by the neck, forcing him back on his knees.

"Please, Dad. Please. Let go …" He is begging in choked whispers, his eyes blinking back a steady stream of tears.

I am weeping uncontrollably. Not because I pity myself, but because in these moments of terror, I am bewildered and wondering why it is happening. *Why does he beat us? Why does he hate us so much, his own flesh and blood? Why does he long to feel us quake beneath his hands and beg for his mercy?* Quiet sobs shake my body. Fear catches in my throat.

My brother pleads with him. "Please. Please stop!"

"Shut up! Don't talk! Who told you you could talk?"

My dad sees me crying. I cry for my brothers because even in their pain they are looking for his love, hoping to find it somewhere in the painful blows and curses. I don't look for that love. I simply let my hatred of him wash over me and strengthen me, steeling myself for what is coming.

"Why are you crying? I haven't touched you. Don't be a baby! I'll beat you just for crying." The hard whack of his hand stings against my skin. I gasp for air. Another slap to the side of my neck sends me sprawling to the floor. I try to tuck into myself and make myself small. He is frenzied, getting in as many hits as he can. We are weeping out loud now. All of us. I try to bite back any noise, knowing it infuriates him, but a vicious slap to my face causes my lip to begin bleeding and a wail of agony escapes my lips.

He stands above us, his fury exhausted. "You are all nothing. You never will be. Get in bed."

My dad likes to follow up his blows with insults, wounding our already-fragile spirits. In some twisted way, we know he wants to be proud of us, to look at us and think better of himself, but his constant degradation has robbed us of our will to thrive and the ability to be confident. We are barely surviving at this point.

"You are all raised by dogs. You are a bunch of useless idiots." With that, he turns and walks out the door.

Whimpering softly, we pick up the nightclothes he ripped off of us hours earlier and gingerly step into them. I move slowly, trying not to make any noise.

"Roger?" My dad calls to me down the dimly lit hallway. His voice is smooth and even, as if nothing has happened. As if he has not shredded our bodies and our self-worth with a stick and the poison of his words. "Roger, come here."

Every so often, my dad calls me to him after beating us. My stomach flip-flops and my breathing quickens. I hate these moments more than the beatings. Swiping at the blood on my lip with the back of my hand, I walk slowly out into the hallway.

My dad is sitting in front of the television, the screen flickering, casting weird shadows on the wall. A cigarette smolders in the ashtray on the coffee table.

My mom is nowhere in sight. She is always absent when the beatings happen. Her absence proves her neglect of us. She is never there when we so desperately need a protector, a comforter, a piece of hope to cling to.

"Come here." He holds his arms out to me.

If I could turn and run, I would. I walk to him. He folds me in his arms, pulling me onto his lap. A cool hand caresses my hair. I feel the stubble of my father's cheek against the smoothness of my own.

"I love you, Roger. You know that, don't you?"

I barely nod.

He rubs my thigh. "Don't ever forget that I love you."

He turns and kisses my ear, letting the tip of his tongue trace its outline. My stomach churns, and I pull away from the sourness of his breath. At this, he holds me tighter. Everything about him repels me—the sound of his voice, the smell of his cologne, the way he nuzzles my neck. I feel myself go numb and think about the tree outside my room that shades our walled garden. I long to climb to its highest leafy branch and fly away from here.

Finally, he pushes me off his lap. "Go to bed."

Angry tears spill down my face as I slip down the hall. Every fiber of my body cries out three little words: *I hate you. I hate you. I hate you.*

Flipping on the bathroom light, I run warm water over my hands. Lathering a bar of soap, I scrub at my face and neck and ear. The warmth of the water does nothing to soothe me. I can't seem to get the stink of his cologne off me. I wash my face again and again, my angry tears mixing with the suds slipping down my cheek.

I know my mother hears me in the bathroom, but even now she doesn't come. I am alone in this house of pain. The eyes that stare back at me from the mirror are red-rimmed and filled with hate. Someday I will be free of him. Of them. But tonight I can only crawl back into my bed knowing tomorrow will bring more of the same.

The sense of hopelessness that fills our childhood home permeates everything we do. We breathe it in. We are mired in it, not knowing if we will ever be free.

■ ■ ■

The morning's brightness is harsh and piercing. A fly is stuck in the crack of the open window in our bedroom, buzzing at the screen. I have been awake for an hour, heart pounding and stomach churning. In a few hours we will be at school. Another torture I must endure every day.

Rolling over in bed, I gaze out the window. No sign of rain clouds. I always hope for a huge thunderstorm to keep us home from school.

I push back the covers at the sound of my mom's voice. She calls from her room, waiting for us to get our own breakfast and lunch. "Boys! Get up! You are going to be late for school. I will tell your father if you are late. You know what he will do to you."

We are up, moving, dressing quickly despite last night's bruises. Our mom often uses the promise of our dad's beatings to motivate us. She knows the pain of his cruelty herself, yet she doesn't spare us. She could shield us from him or run away with us somewhere. Somewhere safe. Instead, she encourages him in his rages when it is to her advantage. It baffles me how someone could invite cruelty on her own children.

Her voice rings out again from her bed. "Don't make me tell your father. That would be a shame."

There is an uneasy peace in the house after my dad leaves for China Airlines each day. The air seems lighter when he is at work, but there is no comfort from my mother. Under her beauty, she is hard and unyielding.

Looking back, I know now that she was a woman filled with pain and insecurity. Her marriage was a nightmare and her life was a disappointment. But she could never push past her own needs to love us. We suffered daily from her neglect and her cruel manipulations and were left to fend for ourselves.

We are not poor. We have a large home with a huge garden, but there is nothing in the house for breakfast. Stomachs growling, we rummage through the kitchen to find something for our lunch. Leftover rice and soggy vegetables are all we find. I feel tears prick my eyes. I already know I will be too embarrassed to pull out this lunch in front of my schoolmates.

Shoving our lunches in our book bags, we head for the front door. My oldest brother pushes past us angrily. "Get out of my way!"

My other brother clutches at his shoulder as the pain from last night's bruising is newly awakened. "You're a jerk."

They are always at each other, but we follow him out the door. I bring up the rear, tucking in my white shirt and adjusting the belt on my uniform. The screen door slams behind me, marking our exit. There is no good-bye kiss for us, no hug before we go off to school. My mother keeps her affections for the younger children. We are on our own.

A wall of humid air greets us as we walk down the sidewalk. The promise of rain hangs in the air, but it never comes. Bustling city traffic stops and starts, waiting at crosswalks as clusters of uniformed girls and boys make their way to school. Exhaust fumes mix with the smell of hot tar from the new pavement the street workers are laying.

Even with the loud rumble of the construction crew's machine, a quiet stillness settles over me. This is my favorite time of the day. The rhythm of the walk and the time by myself anchors me. A brief ribbon of peace that separates the cruelty of home and the chaos of school.

My brother's long legs quicken our pace. "Hurry up! You are going to make us late!"

I skip to keep up.

The brother who is closest to me in age jostles by me, prodding me in the ribs. "Don't make us late!" He mimics our older brother, matching his stride.

I try to stretch out the walk to school as long as I can, but I don't want to be late either. The last time I was late, the dean showed up, pulling me to the front of the class, saying, "This is what happens when you are late." He'd grabbed the front of my hair, bringing tears to my eyes, and lopped off odd sections of my hair with a pair of scissors. All day I'd sat with patchwork hair, hearing the snickers of my classmates.

School is a different torment than home, but it is a torment just the same. Thinking of that painful day, I run my hand over the roughness of my hair. A ripple of anxiety works its way through my stomach. I begin to jog. The squat structure of the school, framed by trees, is just in sight.

The school day passes in a blur.

My mind is numb with facts. The hard wood of the chair presses against the backs of my knees. A math paper rests beneath my hot palm. The teacher, her black hair hanging like a curtain over the side of her face, slips between the desks, knuckles wrapped around a pair of chopsticks. The smoothness of her features masks a hidden cruelty that is exposed when one of her students doesn't meet her expectations. A small drop of sweat runs down my cheek, plopping on my paper, and I quickly brush it off. I wish I were smarter or brighter or that my schoolwork would come easily to me.

I keep my head down, looking at my work to escape her attention. My classmate is not so lucky. At the sight of a wrong answer on his sheet, the teacher grabs at his fingers with her chopsticks, twisting his fingers violently. He cries out, like a small boy, even though he is ten. The class is still, barely breathing. She yanks him from his seat. His feet tripping over each other, she drags him to the front of the class. With a cruel shove, she has him kneeling at the front of the class, facing us.

"I have never seen such a stupid boy. A five-year-old could have gotten that answer right. You will stay here until school is out. Maybe that will help you remember to not be stupid." She pokes at him with her chopsticks.

I don't look at him. I know I will see tears in his eyes. I know this because it is what happens to me when the teacher makes me kneel. If I could wish the rest of the day away for him, I would. As it is, I refocus on my paper, rechecking each of my answers so that I will not have to join him.

The cruelty we experience on a daily basis from the teachers who are supposed to be shaping our minds and thoughts and growing us as individuals is unthinkable. The daily humiliation we find at school does not lend itself to a love for learning. We are in fight-or-flight mode, barely surviving.

My brothers meet me after class, and we begin the walk back home. As we veer off down another crowded street, a steady stream of people push past us. An older boy, with a sneer on his face and a book bag slung over his shoulder, shoves me out of his way. A pretty teenage girl is laughing with a boy, a cold bottle of soda in her hand. Their heads are close together as they walk down the sidewalk.

"Where are we going?"

"Grandma and Grandpa's. They are out of town."

A wide smile lights my face. My mom's parents started a large insurance company in Taipei when they fled Canton during the rise of Mao Zedong. Their beautiful home, with its spacious halls and countless rooms, is our favorite afternoon playground.

As we wind down the side streets, the houses get larger and grander. Groves of trees shade the mansions. Flowers grow in profusion, lining porches and creeping up trellises. The nervous energy of the city streets dissipates into the quiet calm of the upper-class neighborhood. The afternoon sun hangs like an orange globe in the sky, heating the pavement and beating down on our dark heads as we make our way to their house.

We turn up the sidewalk. I push at my damp hair with my hand. A trickle of sweat slips between my shoulder blades. Our oldest brother walks up to the massive front door and knocks. We are lost in the shadow of its frame. A few minutes pass.

My other brother leans in closely, his hands cupped against the door to listen. "They are in there! I can hear them. Knock again!"

We pound harder at the door. Again we wait, minutes ticking by, the sound of a nearby fountain trickling in the background.

"Let us in! We know you are in there."

There is the click of the lock and finally the wide door opens, revealing a steely-eyed servant girl and a deep, cool hall that beckons us. The open hostility our grandparents' servants have for us is borrowed from our grandparents' attitude toward us. I long to be close to my grandpa, who seems kind and tenderhearted, but my grandma reminds me of my mother—cold and calculating. On the whole, they both ignore us, trying to make us feel smaller than we already feel. But that never stops us from trying to wring as much enjoyment as we can in the moments we are free from the hardship of both home and school.

We don't wait to be invited in. We rush past the servant, laughing, thankful for the coolness and the open space to run free.

"Don't touch anything, you crazy boys. Your grandparents are not here. No running!" she calls after us as our feet slap the tile in our attempt to escape her. The anxiety of the day and the fear of going home slips from my mind.

"Hide and seek!"

My brothers run ahead. We like to play for hours. There are so many rooms. The only rooms I stay away from are the rooms with the idols and pictures of gods. When we have been here at night, their fierce eyes, lit by candles, and the heavy smell of incense filling the rooms have given me nightmares.

I scurry down the hall toward a large sitting room. The servants try to keep an eye on us, but we are quick and hide before they can corner us. Sometimes our mother asks us to pocket trinkets or money that we find in the house to bring back to her, but today I am here to play. To forget. To lose myself in the luxury and largeness of this space.

I look back over my shoulder and hold my breath. No one is looking. I tiptoe into a room filled with ornate furniture, glad to lose myself in the game. I sneak into a corner and hide myself behind a weighted, blue silk curtain framing the window. *They will never find me in here.* I hear the patter of feet. Pressing my hands against the coolness of the wall, I will myself not to move.

Two of the servant girls are talking. I can't see them, but their words pierce through the heavy cloth.

"What are those brats doing here?"

"Probably here to steal some pocket money again."

One snorts.

"I guess we should feel sorry for them. Their mother is so beautiful. She is so fair. But I have seen her black-and-blue when she has come here to escape *him*." She spits out my father's name.

My eyes start to burn. I rub them with the backs of my hands.

"I heard that he beat her the night of her wedding. Is that true?"

"Who knows. Probably. All I know is we need to get those kids out of here before they break something or take something else."

Their voices fade as they move into another room.

There is no place we can go to escape the shame of my father and what he does, or the neglect of my mother and how she chooses not to shield us from him. Not even the cool elegance of our grandparents' home.

■ ■ ■

Later that night, I crawl into bed, under a thin sheet. The room is dark and damp with humidity. My brothers are already asleep. We do not know what the night will hold for us. We hope for sleep. The warm air presses against me. The low murmur of my dad's voice grows louder in the living room. There is a shattering crash of glass. Curses roll down the hall and fill our room. He sounds close. Too close.

A tight knot begins to form at the base of my throat. Once again hot tears squeeze through my tightly shut eyes. I grip the sheet and whisper a prayer, hoping that a God I have never met will hear me. *Is this it for this life? When I die, where do I go? Is it just this darkness?*

My mom cries out. There is another crash.

Is it?

All I have ever seen, all I have ever known, is darkness. The darkness of abuse and rejection. The darkness of fear and hopelessness. The uneven footsteps are coming closer. I turn to face the wall, willing the footsteps away, my heart butterflying against my chest. The darkness closes in.

■ ■ ■

I had no idea that my cry in the dark took wing, on that black night, to the Creator of light. I didn't know that, even then, God's hand was upon me and that He was making a way for me that would take my family halfway around the world to America. I didn't know these things. But something was stirring in heaven on my behalf. Hope was coming.

This childhood memory fades and another takes its place.

I am seventeen and angry.

It seems like yesterday.

Chapter 3

BREAKING FREE

San Francisco, 1973
Nothing is easy in life. The choice is yours.

Opening the front door of our two-story row house, I step forward, filling its frame. The late-afternoon sun warms my aching muscles. Shading my face with my hand, I look out across the street toward the wide green lawns of Golden Gate Park and the groves of eucalyptus trees that frame the grass. Frenzied bongo music pulses and fills the air with its rhythm, and college kids and teenagers are everywhere—on the grass, walking down the sidewalk, clustered around blankets, talking and laughing. School is out. Under a lone cypress tree, a group of kids surrounds the bongo player, dancing and swaying, matching their movements to its beat.

We've been here for two years, and I still can't get used to all the white faces. San Francisco is nothing like Taipei. There are a million different sounds and smells. Even the air feels different. It is a summer day, but there is no humidity and the air is cool. My T-shirt and jeans would have clung to me with sweat if I were at a park in Taipei during the summer months. Here the sun warms the gravel walking paths, and people lounge on the park benches while a light breeze blows in off the bay.

A young boy in cutoff shorts shouts as he tosses a Frisbee to a fluffy brown dog. A teenage girl with braids runs after the dog, yelling his name. A hippy couple sitting on a blanket playing their guitars strums a tune I've never heard before. I can barely make out the melody.

They all look so happy, so sure of themselves ... like they belong.

There is an ache in my chest. I wish I were out on the grass. I wish I belonged with them, with their music and their laughter.

This theme of loneliness loomed around me throughout my entire childhood and young adulthood, separating me from the joy and relationship I craved. It shadowed my thoughts, affected how I moved and how I interacted with others. I was alone both physically and emotionally.

I hear the shrill hum of my mother's voice in the kitchen. Oil sizzles in the pan. The smell of garlic browning wafts from the kitchen. Looking over my shoulder, I see my younger brother and sister sitting at the table. Being the youngest, they are my mother's favorites. I used to try to get her attention, craving her hugs and kind words, but those days are over. The long years of neglect have pulled me from her manipulative grip. I don't love her. I can't get far enough away from her now.

I lean up against the doorframe and wince. Last night's bruises are fresh and the pressure smarts. One thing hasn't changed since China Airlines transferred my dad to San Francisco. The beatings still happen every day. We brought that hell with us to our strange, new country.

Two years have gone by since we arrived in San Francisco. Two years of struggling to make English words come out of this Chinese mouth. Two years of keeping my thoughts and my words to myself as I made my way down the corridors of George Washington High without being bothered. Two years of being a loner.

I still haven't found a group of friends to fit into. I don't want to hang out with the other immigrant kids. They group themselves together like a small island, keeping to themselves, speaking Chinese, and dressing oddly. I want to be like the cool American kids with their bright laughter and easy confidence, but my accent and nervousness show me for who I am.

My cousins, who live in Tiburon and have new clothes and polished English, just laugh at us. When we'd moved here, I thought that at least they would be our friends. When we'd first arrived, I loved staying at their large home with its wide view and beautiful interior. All of America seemed to be at our fingertips. But we outgrew our welcome after a month. Like the rest of my mom's family, they, too, were eager to get us out of their hair so they could get on with their lives.

I exhale a deep, slow breath through pursed lips and rub the back of my neck with my hand. Maybe it will be better now that I've graduated from high school. Maybe turning seventeen will mark a golden year—the year that I will find some friends and some moments of peace.

Traffic is backed up in front of the house. A purple Datsun cuts off a Cadillac. There is some honking and gesturing. People are coming home from work, tired and ready for dinner. They are not as laid-back as the kids who hang out at the park. This is my cue to go up to my room, before my dad's car makes its way down Fulton Street toward the house.

When we'd first arrived, my dad had continued his work as an in-flight controller, managing all the liquor that made it onboard for the passengers. His temper and leanings toward bribery lost him that job. He'd pooled his substantial resources and bought a corner grocery store. The pressures of owning his own business seem to fuel his already outrageous anger. Dinnertime seems to be his favorite time to explode. My stomach tightens with anxiety.

Taking two steps at a time, I start to head up the stairs. But it's too late. The show has started. My dad has always been great at making a scene.

The front door slams against the wall. Turning, I see him, hands clenched at his sides, stalking toward the kitchen. Who knows what has set him off this time. One too many drinks? A gambling debt hanging over his head? A rude customer hassling him at the store?

He sees me climbing the stairs. "Get over here! Where do you think you are sneaking off to?" The easy flow of curses slip from his lips like water.

I can't ignore him. That only makes him more furious and the beatings more brutal. I know what is in store for me. I turn on my heel and slowly walk back down the stairs. He mutters under his breath. I can feel the heat of his simmering anger come off him as I follow him into the kitchen.

Out of the corner of my eye, I notice my siblings shrink down close to the table. The fear owns us all, even the little ones. Hearing us come in, my mom turns from the stove. A hint of anxiety flushes her cheeks. She knows his moods by the set of his mouth and the look in his eyes. She knows what is coming. I move beside her. The common beatings are the only things that connect us. We have faced this same scenario a hundred times. It always ends with tears and blood.

"Dinner is almost ready," she says quietly, as if the promise of steaming rice and savory vegetables will subdue him.

At the sound of her voice, his rage is uncorked. With a yell, he surges toward her, hand raised.

Without thinking, I press my hand against his chest, holding him at arm's length. We are eye to eye. Flecks of spit gather at the corners of his mouth. He tries to push forward, but we are both surprised by my strength. The heat of adrenaline and hatred surge through me. I am impenetrable.

"Get out of my way!" he screams at me, reaching for my mom, who is frozen in her astonishment. My stance holds. My strength matches his.

"No!" I yell back at him.

He looks at me as if he is seeing me for the first time. My anger. My power. My hatred. As my hand digs into his chest, a greater anger than I have ever felt before in my life rips through me. An accumulation of rage at the years of torture, neglect, and humiliation at the hands of my father thrums through my body, bringing a new clarity to my thoughts. In that moment, staring at each other, my dad and I both know one thing: if he tries to push past me, I will kill him.

He sags against my hand and I push him away.

"You'll never amount to anything! You are nothing! A nobody!"

His words roll off of me. They are nothing new. He has said them to me a million times before. I just stare at him. Straight in the face. This is a new thing. Unused to being challenged, he turns, cursing, and leaves the kitchen.

The kitchen is silent with surprise. My mom places a hand on my hot shoulder. I shrug it off. "Don't."

The last thing I want is her touching me. I didn't do this for her. I don't want her to think she is forgiven. She isn't. I still don't understand why she never stood up for us, why she let our dad torment us for years. That is something that will never make sense to me.

Heading out of the kitchen, a sense of euphoria overtakes me. I faced down the devil and I won.

One thing is clear. I won't stay in this nightmare another day, another hour, another minute. Not one more moment will be spent sweating with the fear of knowing that a bruising blow is coming. Not one more tear will be cried over the fresh humiliation of not being loved and cared for. Nothing can hold me here. The fear of all my father can do to me is gone.

I don't bother to think about what my leaving will do to my mother. She is on her own. I have nothing to tie me to my family. I don't even know what a family is.

I push open the front door and head down the steps, drawing in huge breaths of the soothing evening air as if I am breathing for the first time in my life. My feet slap the driveway with a newfound intensity. I can't get out of there fast enough. All my hopes have come true in one moment. My thoughts tumble over each other. *I am free. Free. No more screaming. No more beatings. No more explosive dinners.*

My stomach grumbles. I hear my name.

"Roger? Roger!"

I turn. My mom is running down the driveway after me.

"Where are you going?" Lines furrow her forehead above her nose. She rubs her knuckles with her hand. She is worried. But I have seen that look before. I have heard that note of concern sharpen her voice. It is not concern for me. She reserves her worry for herself.

I shrug. "I don't know where I'm going, but I'm not staying here."

I see the finality of my statement bring her chin up. There is no love for me in her eyes, no regret turning down her mouth with sadness. She simply turns and heads back to the house.

Taking the keys from my pocket, I get into my '76 Camaro and pull out onto Fulton. None of my brothers or sisters come to the window. No one beckons me back. I take a breath and let it out. Dinner is calling. This is going to be the best dinner I have ever had.

It isn't until I am three bites into my burger at the Doggie Diner that my newfound happiness dips and wavers. The fast-food joint is full. Fluorescent lighting casts a bright-yellow hue over the booths. The murmur of dinner talk fills the diner, and I glance around and take in the customers. A few cops are chatting in the corner over their pastrami sandwiches. A young family with a squirming toddler and a baby stroller stand at the counter ordering French fries. In the corner booth, a long-haired girl and her clean-cut boyfriend are sharing a shake, intertwining their fingers across the table.

Everyone here is with someone. Everyone here has someone to talk to and a place to go home to when they leave. Everyone, that is, except me.

A new fear anchors me now. The scope of my situation filters into my thoughts.

I am free. It is true. But there is another truth that casts a shadow over my celebration dinner.

I am alone with nowhere to go.

■ ■ ■

The colors of this mental image fade and give way to another. Light had started creeping into my darkness. Bursts of color began to frame the black backdrop of my youth. A small piece of hope had begun to wedge itself in my soul.

Love was on its way.

Chapter 4

FINDING A NEW LIFE

San Francisco, 1976
I just called to say I love you.

The sounds in the hotel kitchen at the Fairmont are loud and jarring. The clanks of spoons against pots and calls for pickup fill the room. Oil sizzles in an open pan and puffs of steam escape from a frothy soup pot on the stove. Sous chefs and prep cooks bustle about, leaning over the grill, chopping herbs, tossing pasta, adding garnishes to plates waiting to be picked up. The fragrant smells of beef simmering and garlic warming on the grill are mouthwatering.

No wonder people pay top dollar to eat here.

Tray in hand, I push through the swinging door into the main dining area. Wide white columns separate the tables under a pristine, arced ceiling. Diners sit at cozy tables cloistered behind potted palms, leaning in to talk to each other. The richly carpeted floor mutes the sounds of their conversation. I weave my way between two elderly ladies sipping expensive wine from sparkling glasses and a businessman who's eating alone to a recently emptied table.

The easy chatter of a nearby couple fades into the background as I pick up the delicate plates left on the table. I gently set them on my tray, carefully arranging the silverware so that it won't slip off when I move to the next table. A lipstick-smeared coffee cup shifts on my tray as I quickly load up the discarded napkins and water glasses.

A slim waiter with a quick grin brushes past me and whispers, "You are doing a great job, Roger. Keep it up."

A rush of satisfaction warms my face. I love my new job. It's not every day that a Chinese immigrant is hired at a five-star hotel. I move swiftly toward the kitchen to empty my tray.

The past few years away from my family home have been both a blessing and a curse. I still go by my dad's grocery store to see my family. I always hope for a welcome or a smile, but it is always the same: a glare, a forced hello. Nothing to make me consider moving home. The distance between us has more to do with the disconnect of our souls than the fact that we don't live together anymore. There is too much pain and history that widens the gap between us.

I find myself more at ease the farther away I get from their house. A new vitality fills me that has never been there before. An urge to succeed and live and be more than I am. There is no one breaking me down with cruel words or hardened fists. I come and go as I please. Every lungful of air that I breathe is free. Every place I lay my head is a place I have chosen for myself. Every job I take is one step closer to finding a place of peace and a sense of home. I am on a desperate journey to feel safe, to find the peace and the sense of family that have always escaped me.

Sadly, the hilly streets of San Francisco have little to offer in the way of nighttime comfort. A cold, foggy evening can find me huddled in the doorway of a large Victorian home in the Richmond District bracing myself against the creeping wind. It's a safe neighborhood I know well from my junior high paper route. I have also found refuge in the lobbies of high-rise buildings where kind security guards overlook a tired teenager asleep in a chair that's tucked away in the corner.

Summertime is easier. Better yet is when a waitress from one of the many restaurants or hotels where I work gives in to her own loneliness and invites me over for the night. At least then I have a bed. A pillow for my head. A hot shower to clean up in after a long day of busing and serving. There is not a lot of emotion involved. We both know this is nothing more than a way to pass the night. In the morning it is off to work. As long as I'm on time and work hard, my bosses could not care less where I sleep. My lack of a bed, of a home, of a person to love who will love me back just reinforces the sense that I am truly alone, left to make my way in a strange place in a hard time.

I have left a trail of jobs behind me, taking two or three at a time to fill my pockets and the emptiness of my days. The Starlight Room restaurant at the Sir Francis Drake Hotel. Paprikas Fono in Ghirardelli Square. Max's on the Square at Geary and Mason. Nautilus on Pier 39. The Ferry Plaza restaurant, most recently called the World Club, that sits on the water overlooking the Bay Bridge. I am working my way up. Making a success of myself. I prove my father wrong each time I succeed. I am driven by loneliness and the unquenchable desire to make something of myself. I need to find a home for my restless soul. I will do it. There is no one who can stop me now.

The clink of silver on china brings me back from my reverie. Pausing at another empty table, I scoop up the used silverware onto my loaded tray and continue my walk to the kitchen.

The waiter who complimented me earlier meets me at the swinging door. "Hey, a few of us guys are heading out to a new club tonight. Good music. Drinks. Fun. Wanna come?"

I shake my head. "Not tonight, Mike, but thanks. Maybe next time."

He shrugs. "Sure. You know we like you, Roger. Anytime you want to come, you are welcome."

I smile at him again. It is good to have friends.

I dropped out of City College after one lonely, depressing, mind-numbing year and immersed myself in the hotel-restaurant scene. I found camaraderie with my coworkers that I never had with my classmates. All my friendships are hard-won. I don't take them lightly. As the years pass, an ache for companionship forms an unfillable pit in my gut. I need more than a strange bed and a midnight connection with a random girl. A need for a hand to hold and an ear to listen grows in me. Even with these hotel friends, I still feel alone. It seems crazy to hope for someone to love me. But something in me still craves the family I have never had. And someone I met on a cool summer day has made me feel like it is possible.

In the kitchen I pause to separate the silverware from the dinner plates. Unloading dishes is mindless work. My thoughts turn to the beautiful girl with twinkling brown eyes and the profusion of curly brown hair who has turned my life upside down. I close my eyes and I am back in that moment of first glimpsing my future.

■ ■ ■

The pavement in front of my dad's corner grocery store is lined with cracks. Tracing a large seam in the concrete with my shoe, I lean against the brick of the building, sucking in a deep breath off a newly lit cigarette. The scent of the smoke calms me. I always feel on edge being around my family. A cool breeze lifts the hair off my collar. I can hear my dad talking at the register when a dark-haired customer in a jean jacket opens the door and enters the grocery. As the door swings shut, I see his car parked at the curb. Inside, is a girl. *The girl.*

Bare feet up on the dash and a bare, brown arm resting on the window, her head is thrown back against the headrest. Paul Anka is crooning "Put Your Head on My Shoulder" on the radio. Its melody filters through the window.

She leans her head out the window and our eyes meet. Her brown eyes are lit from within with a warm friendliness. Tucking a stray curl behind her ear with a tanned hand, she looks at me and breaks into a wide grin. A wide grin for me. A full smile for the lonely boy smoking away his uneasiness outside his dad's store. That smile takes me in and fills me up in one second. Paul Anka is singing the song of my soul as I look at her.

Tossing my cigarette to the ground, I am next to the car, leaning down, drinking in the sight of her, hoping for more than her smile. "Hi, I'm Roger. What's your name?"

Her painted toes keep time to the music on the dash. "Maite."

"Okay. Maite. That is a very pretty name. I have never heard it before."

"I know. It's different. It's Basque," she explains.

"I like it … a lot." I smile back at her.

She laughs. That sound wrenches something free inside me. Her hand rests against the warm metal of the doorframe. I place mine next to hers.

"Listen … I'm wondering … Could I have your number?"

The breeze catches one of her curls as she looks at me, amused.

The driver comes out of the store behind me. I hear him before I see him. He walks around to the driver's door. Pushing his sunglasses up on his head, he takes me in with a grin. We have seen each other around the store before. I find out later that he is Maite's brother, Michael. Maite turns toward him as he slides into his seat and takes the cold Coke bottle, beaded with condensation, out of his hand.

"What do you think?" I ask again. The car's engine revs impatiently.

"Sure," she says, shrugging her shoulders. A flush of pink colors her cheeks. "Why not?"

Dropping her feet to the floor, she takes a slip of paper and pen from her purse and scribbles down her number.

"Come on, Maite. Let's go," says the driver. His head is cocked to the side, but he humors her, letting her palm the number to me. Our fingers brush.

"See you later, Roger."

I step back from the car as it pulls away from the curb. I raise my hand, lifting up her number. "I'll call you. Nice to meet you, Maite."

She lifts her arm in a wave, her laughter floating back to me on the breeze.

"I'll call you!" I call after her. Something in my world just shifted with that smile.

I only wait one hour to call her. I know a good thing when I see it.

■ ■ ■

"Roger, there are three tables that need busing."

Shaking off my thoughts, I snatch up my tray off of the counter.

"Thanks, Mike." I nod to him and quickly walk past him. It's good to have someone looking out for me. Pushing through the door, I take in the dining room, noting the tables I need to clear. The girl with the bright smile still crowds my thoughts.

■ ■ ■

Two hours after I meet Maite, I pull the Camaro up in front of her house on Ninth Avenue and get out of the car. It is a pretty house, set back on a wide, front lawn—a rarity in San Francisco. She is standing on her porch, hands on her hips and an incredulous look on her face. She is lovely and slim in bell-bottom jeans and a leather blazer.

"What are you doing here? I just met you. I don't even know you."

Hands in my jeans pockets, I lean against the hood of my car and shrug. "I just thought you might like a ride to work."

"I told you on the phone that I can get myself to work, Roger."

"Why not let me take you? I am here."

I see a smile begin to play at the corners of her mouth.

"You really are persistent, aren't you?"

I just grin at her.

Folding her arms across her chest, she looks at me. The stern lines on her forehead give way to the creases of her smile. She laughs, shaking her head. She is beautiful when she laughs. If she will let me, I will try to make her laugh every day.

"Okay. Wait here. Let me say good-bye to my kids and talk to the babysitter."

She goes inside. I hear voices as she comes back to the porch. The voices of children. A girl with a mass of curls follows Maite outside and reaches up to wrap both arms around her waist, burying her face in Maite's side. A shorter boy with a snub nose snuggles his head on her shoulder as she bends to hug him. She kisses them both several times. She seems like a wonderful mother. My heart aches a little at the sight of them.

Love. Family. Happiness. I know it in my heart even though I have never experienced it. Seeing these gentle hugs and the exchange of affection between mother and children is like a salve to my bruised soul.

Maite whispers in her kids' ears, squeezing them one more time, and sends them back inside before picking up her purse. I am a sideline observer, but in that moment, Maite brings a belief in a new kind of life with her as she makes her way down the stairs toward my car.

"Here you go." I open the door for her and close it behind her.

"Thanks for taking me to work, Roger. This is very sweet."

Again the kindness in her face fills me with a surge of happiness. If hope could take on human form, it would have a wide smile and brown curls.

Getting behind the wheel, I take a deep breath and start up the car. I am smiling. I can't help myself.

■ ■ ■

In the dining room of the Fairmont, filling my tray with water glasses, I find myself smiling again just thinking about Maite. *She is changing my life. She is changing me.* Her smile, her words, her gentleness are a warming light in the cold darkness of my life.

Sitting in the seat next to her, something monumental shifts inside of me.

No longer am I alone, searching for love and wholeness. For the first time, someone meaningful has walked into my life. She is not a fling or a one-night stand. I am put at ease by her kindness and her grace. With her, I am not just the lonely, rejected boy from Taipei. I have a purpose and a dream. To be with her.

The sound of her words and the warmth of her smile fill my soul. The joy and peace that wash over me are new sensations. I have never had this kind of feeling before. All the sad songs about loving and leaving someone that have defined my relationship experience slip away. The fantasy of being with someone is now embodied by Maite when she sits next to me in my car.

I've only had an hour with her, but I know I want to be with her forever.

■ ■ ■

I had no clue, as I cleared tables and swept crumbs from white linen tablecloths, how completely Maite's love would alter my life. The warmth of what she brought and still brings to my world can't be quantified. How can I express the largeness of the gift she graced me with when she chose to love me? I didn't know how to love her back. My capacity to engage and flourish in a relationship had been stunted by the countless rejections and horrors of my childhood. I had been love-starved for so long, I took all I could from her but didn't know how to return that life-giving warmth.

Even though we had found each other, we loved each other in fits and starts, breaking up and making up. We were both still missing a deeper, richer love that we needed to ground us in our life together. A wide stream of grace that would anchor us in our journey of marriage and family.

The pictures of my busboy days fade in my mind as my memories shift to those early years of our marriage. And to beautiful Maite of the wide smile and compassionate heart, the one who loves so well and so completely, who is about to lead me on the greatest adventure of my life.

The next memory looms before me like a lantern on a wire, glowing with the warmth of a new light that is beginning to flood our lives.

Chapter 5

FINDING SALVATION

San Francisco, 1983
How deep is Your love.

I let myself into the apartment with my key. The living room is warm with the late-afternoon sun, its golden tones peeking in through the window shades. Toys litter the floor and a crumpled blanket on the couch beckons me, inviting me to soak up its warmth. The smell of this morning's coffee, still in the pot, lingers in the air. No one is home. Maite's work as a hairstylist keeps her busy while I am auditing at the Marriot. She swings by to pick up the kids from her mom on her way home from work every day. I only have a few hours before the joy and chaos of four kids hits our two-bedroom apartment. This is my moment of peace. A fleeting moment of rest, in between my two auditing jobs, when I try to rejuvenate myself.

I wouldn't trade my auditing work for anything. The move from restaurant worker to auditor-in-training a few years earlier at the Crowne Plaza Hotel was just the break I needed to launch me on a new path to success. I don't take any opportunities for learning and growing for granted.

Still, sleep is highly underrated. I would kill for a few more hours to let a little relaxation work its way into my bones. The few hours of sleep I get in the early evening is all I have to keep me going through the graveyard shift at the Crowne. I live this life of family and work fueled by coffee and make-up naps on the weekends. This is a pattern I will keep going for a long time. Thoughts of failure or losing a job keep me doubling up on jobs.

I run my hand through my hair, pausing to rub the back of my neck. A creeping weariness works its way down from my fingertips to the soles of my feet. Thoughts of work and life flood my mind as I glance around the room. Thoughts about all the projects I have in front of me.

My work life is fast-paced and full. I spend more time with my fellow auditors than I do with my wife and kids. I can't forget to touch base with my boss about working a few more hours. Every dollar in the bank makes me feel safer and a little more sure of myself.

The pressure of a full family life at home never leaves me. And marriage. This partnership that has woven itself into the mesh of my life.

Why can't I love Maite like I should?

My hard knot of a heart is still tangled up in the fear and pain of the past. I am always afraid she will abandon and reject me like my mother did. Some things don't change so easily.

I press the heels of my hands against my eyes and let out a long sigh. *I just need to rest.*

I clear a place for myself on the couch, tossing a rumpled doll and some Matchbox cars to the floor. Squeezing in quality time with four children between two full-time jobs isn't something I've mastered either.

I shake my head, trying to clear it. I can't relax with all these thoughts tumbling around in my head. Maybe a little television will lull me to sleep faster. Flipping on the TV, I turn to arrange the pillows on the couch and then slide down, feeling its familiar form. Letting out a deep sigh, I feel the muscles in my neck start to relax. Sleep will not be long in coming.

As usual, Maite has left the channel on some Christian show. My French Catholic wife has gotten religion. I see one of the Jesus pamphlets that she brings home tucked under the *TV Guide* on the coffee table.

I run my hand through my sun-warmed hair again, remembering the scene that took place in our living room the past Sunday morning.

Maite was at the door holding Christian, our squirming toddler, in her arms. Michelle's small hand was pulling at Phil's. He bent down to tickle her, and she squealed with delight. Marie France rested her hand on Maite's shoulder. My two lovely girls with curly brown hair. *Since when have they been the same height?* The years are slipping through our fingers like beach sand. The teenage years are upon us.

"Are you coming with us, Roger?"

I shook my head. "No, sorry. I'm going to stay home today." I crave any time I can get alone. I've gone a few times to appease Maite, but I find it's easier to sleep on the couch than on a hard, wood pew.

Maite jiggled Christian as he tried to wrench free. "Really, Roger, we would love for you to come with us. The service only goes for about an hour, and we come right home afterward."

I yawned. "I'm exhausted, Maite. You know I try to catch up on sleep on the weekends."

Maite adjusted Chris in her arms. "I know that you work so hard to support our family, but the kids hardly get to see you. This is something we could do together."

I didn't answer her. I just walked into the kitchen. Opening a cupboard door, I took down a coffee cup and filled it to its rim.

"Roger?"

I pulled the milk from the fridge and took a sip from my cup to make room for some.

"Okay, Roger." The sound of resignation was heavy in her voice. "We'll see you when we get home."

I heard the front door open and their voices, big and small, trailed behind them as they headed down the hall.

All her recent talk of church has left me tired. *What is she getting out of it? Don't I give her a good life? Isn't it just one more thing to do?*

She has taken me on a wild religious ride these last couple of years. It all began when she decided that I needed to get baptized. Growing up in the Catholic Church, Maite was taught that divorce and remarrying would keep her from going to heaven. Maite had divorced her first husband before the age of twenty. When she was pregnant with our first child, Michelle, Maite began to panic that we were all going to hell. At least one of us needed to go to heaven. She began pleading with me to get baptized before Michelle was born so that at least I wouldn't go to hell. I'm more concerned about making my mark in this life than worrying about what is going to happen to me in the next. But that's just me. I got baptized into the Catholic Church to put a smile on her face. It was the least I could do for all the smiles she put on mine. But the baptism wasn't enough.

Since then, Maite has gotten sucked in by a slick-talking television preacher promising love and salvation, and she's gone off the deep end. Now it's taking the kids to church every Sunday and cheesy religious programming on the weekends instead of late nights with Johnny Carson.

A sharp, bright note in the hymn playing on TV focuses my thoughts. *When did Maite change? Why didn't I see this coming?*

The craziest thing of all is that something really is changing in her. Right in front of me. A new hope seems to ground her as she navigates our busy life together. She radiates peace. Her smiles are wider and her laughter comes quicker. She is fighting with me less, leaving me to my signature silence when I don't respond to her instead of gauging me with her words or letting her temper flare. I hear her pray for me in our bedroom and I wonder who she is praying to.

Is someone really listening? Does anyone really care about what she is saying? Does anyone up there care about me?

Thoughts of her fade into the noise of the television. *I need some of that peace myself.*

I force my body to relax, stretching myself out the full length of the couch, pulling the blanket over me. My family and two jobs, and the money the jobs pull in, bring a busy fullness to my life, so why am I not happy?

Why am I still scared all the time? I have the family I always dreamed of having. Why am I still looking for something to fill this hole inside of me? Is Maite on to something? Maybe this God of hers is real.

The words of the preacher on the television cut into my thoughts. "You may not know that God loves you, but He does. You may not know that He died for your sins, but He did. You may not know that God has forgiven you, but He has." A tide of emotion is building in his voice, carrying his words into my living room. "Jesus did this for you. For *you*!"

The audience claps with appreciation for his passion.

Despite the heavy exhaustion pinning me to the couch, I'm pulled into the message of the preacher. Somehow, even with his slicked-down hair and Southern drawl, he is drawing me in as he stalks the stage and talks to the camera.

I close my eyes, pressing my eyelids together. *Just go to sleep.*

My few precious moments of rest are eluding me as the voice on the screen challenges me. Urges me to think. I'm drawn in by the power of his words, by the sincerity of his message, by a yawning gap in my soul that is responding to his call.

"There are those of you out there right now, watching this, who need to know that God has never stopped loving you since the day you were born. You have been looking for something your whole life. Wandering around, lost. Trying to fill yourself with anything you can get your hands on. Booze, one-night stands, working your fingers to the bone—and you're running scared. And the worst part is, you still feel empty. You still feel lost and alone."

Eyes open, I toss back the blanket and sit up so I can watch as he talks. This guy is talking to me like he knows me. Like he has lived with me for the past ten years as I've tried to scrape out a good life for myself, shaking off abuse and homelessness, carving out a home and a career for myself. He sees through it all with his truth.

I am lonely. And I'm scared.

Even with Maite, even with four kids, I am driven by the worry of never having enough, of being on the streets again, of fulfilling the prophetic words of my dad that I am nothing and never will be.

I need something more.

I am surprised as tears spill down my cheeks onto the rumpled blanket on my lap.

"God sees you tonight, right where you are, and He is inviting you to begin a new life with Him. He knows you are a sinner. And He loves you anyway. He wants to forgive your sins. His Son, Jesus, died on the cross for you, taking the penalty of your sins, so that you could live in freedom. So that you could have a relationship with the one true God! Your heavenly Father loves you!"

The thought of God as a father loving me pierces my heart—a heart so hardened by pain that I am thwarted in all of my efforts to really love anyone. Even Maite and the kids. A heart so bruised by the rejection of my earthly father that I couldn't really believe anyone would want me ... ever. Especially a holy God.

In a single moment, I realize I am desperate for this love. This love that forgives and erases past grievances. This love that saves and receives the most wounded, sin-filled souls and responds with mercy and grace.

"Won't you say yes to God today? Yes to His love? Yes to His freedom from sin? Yes to a new life in Him?"

"Yes," I whisper, slipping to my knees, my hands wet by tears when they cover my face. "Yes!"

A bright sense of relief spills over me. He loves me. The One who made me loves me and forgives me. This is what I have been craving all along. This is it. This is what Maite meant when she said she was saved. The weight of all my sins, the indifference to my family's need of me, the casual infidelities in my marriage, my selfish way of living, and the coldness I felt toward a God who loves me are being swept away. Somehow the cage of hopelessness that has kept me trapped in despair starts to be unlocked in this moment. Tears of hope slip through my fingers. The tiredness of my body is lost in the physical sense of peace and gratitude that wells up in me.

"Yes!" I whisper over and over, as if each *yes* solidifies the decision I have made to turn my life over to a God I have never known before and yet to the God who has known me and seen me all these long years I have walked the earth.

I get up, brushing the wetness from my face. I am moving, pacing back and forth, in the living room. I'm not quite sure what has just happened. I walk down the hall into the bathroom to wash my face. Hands gripping the rim of the sink, I look at myself in the mirror.

"Yes!"

This is just the beginning.

■ ■ ■

This kaleidoscope of memories fades from dark to light. The brightness of God's love for me seems to bleed into the darkness of my past, tearing me from my most painful memories and leading me forward into the promise of a new kind of living. From Taipei to

San Francisco. From Maite to Jesus. A path of hope leading from my narrowest, darkest moments of despair to the most unimaginable discovery yet. A relationship with a heavenly Father who accepts me—scars and all—and wants to heal me. A God who can take the bitterness of my past and offer the sweetness of His love in its place. A Savior who brings peace in the place of torment and forgiveness to squelch the anger that still lingers within me.

Just like it took me a long time to figure out how to love Maite, it takes me a long time to figure out how to love God. I know His love for me is all encompassing. I know that He has forgiven me. I know that I want Him in my life, but I don't really know what loving Him with my life means. Sitting in church won't do it for me. It's not until the words of a visiting preacher begin to sit in my soul and work their way into my thinking that a life-changing shift comes. The themes of prayer and fasting and chasing after God begin to weave their way into the patchwork quilt of my life, lacing the pain of my past and the hope of my future together. Only prayer and spending time with God can bring about the healing I so desperately long for.

The last memory slips into place like a bright bead upon a string. I am at the beach. And everything is about to change.

Chapter 6

CHASING GOD

Cliff House Beach, 1984
I have nowhere to go but after Him ...

As I make my way down the sandstone cliff toward the ocean, the tang of salty air and the smell of beached seaweed envelop me. Seagulls fight their way against the breeze, riding the air currents in a pattern of lifting and falling. One adventurous bird tucks his bright-white wings against his body and takes a dive, plummeting toward the dipping waves of the Pacific, skimming the water to come up with a small fish in his beak. The cries of the feeding birds circle back to me as my tennis shoes crunch against the sand and pebbles, kick against sturdy clusters of ice plant, and brush the wispy sea grasses that line the winding path.

Behind me is the Cliff House restaurant, a historic landmark that hugs the curve of the cliffs and overlooks the vast expanse of the Pacific Ocean in front of me. A few tourists with cameras around their necks pass me on their way back up the side of the hill. I spot a secluded outcropping of rock directly under the Cliff House and make my way over to it.

Seating myself on the sandy ledge, I take in the full view of the ocean. A few sailboats bob off the coast, their white sails contrasting the hazy strip of the horizon. The sun is warm and large in the sky, having burned off the morning's fog. I love how the wind ruffles the waves under the boats.

I draw a huge breath of beach air into my lungs, then blow it out. It invigorates me. The breaking surf crashes on the rocky beach below me, beating its steady rhythm on the shores.

The beach is my favorite place to come and think and connect with God, whether it's here or going up the coast to Albion to pray and fast at Lord's Land, a retreat spot I have been visiting lately. His creativity and beauty are apparent everywhere here, from the roar of the ocean and the lift of the salty breeze to the jagged cliffs and purple beach flowers that push up between the sandy rocks. I see Him everywhere I look.

The last few years have washed over Maite and me like waves of discovery, layering one on top of the next. Each new experience brings fresh thoughts about God, how much grace He has for us and who He is. In the early days, it was all about changing the way we lived our lives.

I remember walking in from work one afternoon. Maite had a wine bottle in each hand. My eyes widened a little, taking it in.

"Hard day with the kids, Maite?"

She laughed. I joined her.

"No, Roger. The kids are fine. But I was watching a show on the Christian station, and it was talking about how Jesus doesn't like wine. We have to dump out the wine."

The smile quickly left my face. "What do you mean Jesus doesn't like wine? Why doesn't He like wine? Didn't He drink wine?"

Maite was adamant. "We were never meant to be alcoholics. That isn't pleasing to God."

This coming from a French girl.

"Maite, this is some very expensive wine." I wondered if Jesus understood the value of a dollar.

Jesus didn't seem to like rock and roll either, according to Christian television. That revelation had seen the end of my favorite record collection. I shook my head and watched Maite uncork the bottles and pour the lovely purple liquid down the drain in the sink. She was humming. I rubbed my forehead. *Crazy girl. What's next?*

What was next was the immersion into church life and finding new and different ways to serve. More than learning about what we should or shouldn't do according to the latest television program, we were learning who we were supposed to be. Maite was soaking up everything she could find out about this God who loved us so much.

We found a little church in Daly City, a group of people who welcomed us and started us on our Christ-following journey. The second Sunday we were there, the pastor asked for volunteers to help clean the church the following Saturday. Maite had nudged me in the pew. "I can do that, Roger!" She was excited to serve.

Maite walked into the sanctuary the following Saturday. She glanced around, looking for the other volunteers. The sanctuary was empty. She was the only one who had shown up. The pastor's wife smiled gratefully and offered her a bucket and sponge. "Thanks for being willing to clean."

And that was our introduction into church ministry.

Each Saturday we cleaned the church. We vacuumed and cleaned toilets for Jesus.

That was just the beginning.

Maite's love for Jesus and for serving Him was infectious and swept the kids and me along. I was longer in catching on. I was a pew sitter for the first year, catching up on much-needed sleep during the Sunday sermon. But when our pastor asked me to edit videos of a visiting evangelist's sermons on praying, fasting, and spiritual warfare, it set my own journey in motion.

I had volunteered for the media ministry at church and put in hour after hour viewing this visiting pastor's talks and crystalizing his thoughts into a ten-minute blurb to be viewed during church. The thought that God wanted to spend time alone with me was revolutionary. The notion that my prayers, my fasting, could impact the world around me was intriguing.

Now here we are two years later, and our weekends and weeknights are filled with men's ministry, women's ministry, kids' ministry, and media ministry. Between Maite and myself, we juggle seven different ministries. We can't help ourselves in our excitement over learning about how much Jesus loves us.

Our two-bedroom apartment is the church after-party zone. We pack as many people from our church into our living room as we can, serving up snacks, laughing together, leaning into the goodness of God's grace, and enjoying each other's company. We are building a new kind of family, Maite and I. One I have never experienced before. But still there is something missing. It is not enough.

Looking out across the pounding surf, I see the gulls wheeling and swooping on the sea breeze. Their flight seems effortless and masterful, using the wind to their full advantage, to lift them to new heights. *I am ready to fly too.*

I can feel something tugging at my heart. Thoughts working themselves out in my mind. A fervent hope rising in my spirit. I am longing to fast and see God move. To pray and hear back from Him. To fight the spiritual battles that can hold us back if we don't invite God into our circumstances. Who would have thought that a sermon series from a pastor in Fremont could unleash such a longing in me? I have nothing in common with him—except this unassailable urge to connect with the God who loves me. The God who chased me down and found me. I feel a lump forming in my throat and tears prick at my eyes.

"God, I am ready for You to speak to me. I'm listening. Will You speak to me?"

A salty mist rises up from the beach, dampening the air. I breathe it in and wipe at my eyes with the back of my hand. I have started fasting regularly. Praying for God to move in my life and the lives of people around me. Even after repeated weekends of taking men from our church up to pray and fast at Albion, I am still not satisfied. I know it is good; it's not that.

One man's wife came up to me after the last retreat and thanked me. "My husband is a different man. God bless you."

And God is blessing me. Lord's Land has grounded me in these practices of prayer and fasting. I don't know what I am doing, but I know that I need more of God in my life. I want Him to know I am serious about seeking Him.

The moments I spend in Albion in the woods, face lifted toward the beckoning treetops, I can sense Him near. I can feel His pleasure when I press my forehead to the floor of the cabin, telling Him how I love Him and how I need Him more. As I read His words over and over, thumbing through the Gospels and the letters of Paul, I know I am where I am supposed to be, enriching my mind with righteousness and truth. During times of fasting, with a growling stomach and an even hungrier heart for God, a sense of peace and rightness fills me. But I'm still unsatisfied. I want to hear from Him. A specific word. A certain direction that He wants me to go. I want Him to speak to me.

"I'm ready to hear You, God." My words are lost on the breeze.

I rub my palms on my knees, thinking about these past years. Salvation. Church. Family. Ministry. Struggling. Learning. Growing. Stretching. There is a thought that is lingering in my mind. *Maybe God wants more from me.* Maybe I am just scratching at the surface with retreats and video editing and cleaning the bathrooms at church. Maybe I am not looking hard enough or listening long enough for this gracious God who found me and pulled me toward Him to reveal Himself to me.

"Okay, God," I say out loud, my voice catching in the wind. "I know You are real. That You love me. That You have saved me. But I want more, and I want to give You more of myself. I'm going to chase after You. Full-time. I'm not going to hold anything back."

The cries of the seabirds answer me. But there is a fullness in my heart as I stand and head back up the rock-strewn path. It is official. I am going to chase after God with all I have. He's got me.

■ ■ ■

I had no idea what chain of events that prayer, flung to the wind, would set in motion. But like a movie projector flipping through scene after scene and coming to the end of the reel, the memories recede.

I find myself on my face again in my living room, recovering from the heart-wrenching scene in the Tenderloin. Maite is next to me, eyes full of concern, offering tissues, and her arms surround me in a firm hug of comfort as I sit up. The memories of the past years fade, giving way to the present. The living room is cool, and the late-afternoon sun filters through the curtains, casting a pattern on the carpet. I am left with the sense that God has answered my Cliff House challenge in a way I never thought He would.

I said I would chase Him on that windswept cliff a few months earlier. I meant it.

But will I chase Him where He is leading me? Back to the dark streets of the Tenderloin where I left that broken boy? Will I follow Him into the dreary ghettos, the rotten tenements, and the crack houses? Will I follow Him to search out the sin sick and the world weary, the beaten and the bruised, the sorry and forgotten? Will I?

I press my swollen eyelids with the palms of my hands, willing my breathing to return to normal. Warmth spreads through my center, a sense of rightness and purpose steadies my voice as I turn to Maite. "God spoke to me, Maite. I have been asking Him to for so long, and He has finally spoken to me. I'm going back to the Tenderloin. I have to help those people."

She touches my face with a warm hand. "Okay." Her other hand squeezes mine.

I sit in the moment, knowing that I am on the brink of some new thing. A new thing that I could not have dreamed up or thought of on my own. I have no idea what I am going to do or say or how I am going to say or do it. But I know one thing. I am going to the Tenderloin. If that is where God is leading, I am following. He has spoken and His word was clear. The chase is on.

Chapter 7

THE FIRST DAY OF THE
REST OF MY LIFE

Tenderloin, 1984
My life ... my destiny ... my joy ...

Lying on the bed in the early evening hours after my breakdown, I try to relax. I can hear the kids talking in the living room, laughing. Maite is laughing with them. I am always surprised by how easily they find joy. It follows them when they are together.

With only a few hours to rest before my night auditing shift starts at the Marriott, images of the Tenderloin flash through my head. The boy with his head bowed to his attackers. The homeless lady who asked me for spare change. The drug addict passed out in the doorway of the boarded-up bar. The barker selling sex from his strip club. This is the place where God is leading me.

Tossing and turning, I pull the pillow up around my ears, blocking out the sounds in the apartment, a growing excitement pulsing through my veins.

I'm going to need food. That homeless woman was all bones and wrinkles. She looked like she hadn't had a decent meal in months.

Silent prayers layer themselves in my mind.

God, help me. Show me what to do. Where to go. Who to talk to.

Lines from the Lord's Prayer outline that I keep tucked into the pocket of my suit coat weave in and out of my thoughts.

God, let today be the day that I am in Your will. Not doing something I think I should do for You, but doing something You have for me to do.

A plan starts to form in my mind. A nervous excitement tugs at my stomach.

I may not be able to do a lot for the people of the Tenderloin, but I can do something. That is better than nothing.

Turning over on my side, I will myself to sleep. Just a few hours separate me from the coming night shift. Tomorrow will be a new day. My first day in the Tenderloin.

■ ■ ■

The night shift passes by in a blur of computations and columns. My mind is occupied elsewhere. If my coworkers had asked me where my thoughts were, they would have laughed at me. Most people are trying to get out of the ghetto, not get into it. But I have a different plan.

I head back home after my shift with a backseat full of grocery bags. I let myself into the apartment and call out, "Maite! Can you help me?"

She comes out of the kitchen with a cup of coffee. Seeing me, she sets down the cup and grabs a bag out of my arms. "What are you doing with all these groceries? I'm making breakfast right now."

I laugh. "I have to go back down there, Maite. Those people need Jesus … and food." I hoist a bag up onto the counter. "Can you help me make sandwiches?"

Maite fixes her gaze upon me, placing the bag she's holding next to mine, and wipes her hands on a dish towel. She is dressed for the office, looking stylish in a skirt and tailored blouse. She only has a few minutes before she has to leave to drop the kids at school. A faint smile turns up the corners of her wide mouth.

"Sure, Roger. I'll help you make sandwiches."

We form an assembly line. Bread. Bologna. Mustard. Mayo. With each swipe of the knife, I am a minute closer to my destination.

"What are you going to do when you get there?"

"I don't know. Pass out sandwiches. Pray for people."

Maite nods. "Sounds good."

Slipping the last sandwich into a baggie, I squeeze her arm. "Pray for me?"

"Of course!"

I load up the bags with the premade sandwiches and look around the room. "Okay, here I go."

Maite leans in and kisses my cheek. "This is a good thing, Roger." She follows me to the door. "I'll be praying!"

Arms and heart full, I walk down the hall, leaving the warmth of the apartment and the scent of breakfast behind me. I only have a few hours before I am back on at Parc 55. I am going to make each moment count.

Driving down Turk Street, I pull into a parking space at the curb. I open the door and step out onto the sidewalk. My nose crinkles as the raw smells of garbage and urine assail me. The smells are not new to me. Anyone who has lived on the streets is familiar with them, but no one really gets used to them.

I scan the street for someone, as if I will know them when I see them. There is no sign of the boy I saw yesterday or the drug addict I saw lying on the sidewalk.

An older man, bent forward, shuffles past me. His gray hair is matted, and I can see his sock through a hole in the top of his shoe. The stubble on his cheeks is stretched in a frown. I step forward.

"Excuse me, sir."

He scowls at me and keeps shuffling.

"Are you hungry?"

He hesitates and glances at me with a furtive look. "What?"

"Are you hungry? I have some sandwiches I brought ..." My voice trails off.

His body turns and he reaches out a dirty hand toward me. I quickly place a bologna sandwich there. A peace offering for interrupting his walk.

"Thanks," he mumbles, and turns.

"Can I pray for you?" I'm not sure, but I think he starts walking faster. He is not up for a prayer. If only he knew what I know. God will keep chasing him.

It may take a few sandwiches, but the God I am getting to know is relentless. He cares too much to let us keep walking away from Him.

A young girl leaning up against a building with faded red bricks is eyeing me. Her straggly brown hair cascades over her thin shoulders and her tank top reveals swirls of tattoos on her arm. She has seen the exchange. She steps forward.

"Got any more of those sandwiches?"

I quickly put two in her outstretched hand. She looks like she needs more than one. "God bless you."

She squints against the sun. "What are you doing here?"

I shrug. "I was here yesterday. I came back. Can I pray for you?"

She bites her lower lip. "Sure ... and thanks ... for the sandwiches."

"God, bless this girl. You know her and what she needs. Show her how much You love her."

She pulls a sandwich from its plastic film, taking a bite. Dropping the baggie to the ground, she shoves the second sandwich in her bag.

"Come back again," I tell her.

I walk down to the corner of the intersection to a small cluster of homeless men. Cars pass by in a steady stream. A police car is parked by one corner. An officer is talking to a young Cambodian boy in a ratty sweatshirt.

"Hey, would anyone like a sandwich?"

The group of men turns to me and sees the grocery bag in my arms. Gratitude lights their eyes as I press sandwiches into their hands. Their hunger makes us friends. I wonder at their spiritual hunger. How can I break that barrier with them?

More hands are opened as I pass by, into each one I put a sandwich and then I offer to pray for them. Some say yes. Some say no. But it is a beginning. A start.

I look into the empty bag and then at my watch. Fifty sandwiches gone in twenty minutes. I make my way back to the car. I have plenty of time to get to Parc 55 for my next shift. Time for thinking and pondering my next move.

How can I help these people? How can I show them there is hope?

I know God loves them, but how can I convince them of that?

I grin.

One thing is for sure, we're going to need more sandwiches.

■ ■ ■

Saturday morning comes quickly, and a thick layer of fog blankets the peninsula like a heavy quilt. The murky morning sun barely peeks through the curtains. I am awake, restless. I turn and rub Maite's shoulder. "Are you ready?"

"Ready for what?" Her pillow muffles her reply.

"To go pass out sandwiches. I already got more bread. Let's get the kids to help us make them."

I don't wait for her answer. I am up and moving about the room. Something is happening in the marrow of my bones. I feel like I am coming awake for the first time. For so long I have been bent on my own survival. Nursing my own wounded spirit. Cocooned. Keeping to myself with my eyes on succeeding at work. Making sure that I was safe and that my family was taken care of. But in a few short days, it is as if my brain is being rewired to think differently. I don't need extra hours of sleep this morning to catch up on the past week's shortfall. I need to get to the Tenderloin.

I throw open the doors to the kids' bedroom. "Come on, you guys! We are going to make sandwiches and go pass them out in the Tenderloin."

Four sleepy heads start to stir.

Marie France lifts her head from the pillow. "What time is it?"

"It's time to get up! Let's go!"

Her curly head dives back under the covers. Phil doesn't bother to open his eyes. These kids seem to think they need their sleep.

An hour later, with bellies full of breakfast, we are on Eddy Street. I can see a small, gated park from where I stand. The drug addicts are congregating there like it is their own personal playground. Children don't play there. It is too scary. *God, help us. Help them. Help us help them.*

I see Marie France up the street from me. She is shaking off her shyness and handing a sandwich to an elderly woman leaning on her walker. Philip is digging in his bag to reach for more sandwiches, ready to help a young man who is so skinny he looks like he hasn't seen food in a month. Maite is talking to a teenage girl, hand on her shoulder, as she presses a sandwich in her hand and prays for her.

"Hey, can I have one of those?" A man with a patchy beard and soiled clothes approaches me. His eyes are shot with red. I can't tell if he is fifty or seventy. The years ingrained in the lines of his face could be from too many drinks or too many nights slept in frigid doorways. The hand that is held out to me trembles.

"Of course! God bless you. Do you want me to pray for you?"

"I guess so."

I stand close to him. The scent of his unwashed body and dirty hair fills my nose. I keep my face passive. "God, You know this man. Bless him and help him. Be with him today in all that he does. Let him know You love him. Amen."

"Yeah," he says, taking a bite of the sandwich and wiping the crumbs from his face with his hand. "Thanks."

"You're welcome." And I mean it.

Steady traffic moves down the street. Exhaust fumes mix with smells of cooking coming from open windows in the apartments. The drivers look straight ahead. They don't linger in this corner of the city. They are moving through and getting out.

I look at the back of the man retreating up the street, his long hair hanging over his collar, his house shoes shuffling along the dirty sidewalk. I don't want out. I want in. I don't know how, but I won't let one more opportunity to help God's kids pass me by. That is for sure.

■ ■ ■

I couldn't know it at the time, but standing on that cracked pavement, sharing food and simple prayers with people, was tethering me to ground where I stood. God was doing something in me, working a love for those people into my bones. My new passion for Him and knowing Him was being inexplicably connected to a passion for seeing this patch of San Francisco reached by the love of Jesus. A growing conviction was pushing me forward, out of a place of comfort and into a place of service. The hunger for money and security was being replaced by a hunger to set people free.

Maite was on fire. Her passion for Jesus, her desire to do more and more for Him were infectious. We were on a collision course with the destiny God had for us. A destiny of sharing the hope and freedom we were experiencing ourselves with the broken and drifting souls of Eddy Street. The alcoholics who lounged on Jones Street. The porn addicts who frequented the Turk Street peep shows. These were going to be our people. And it was the little ones who would lead the way.

Chapter 8

LET THE LITTLE CHILDREN COME TO ME

Eddy Street, 1984

Passion and compassion

I had no clue how to minister to people in the Tenderloin. Other than bringing in sandwiches and praying with people, I wasn't sure what to do. I didn't have training in missions work. I wasn't a pastor. I wasn't a social worker. I was an immigrant from China who knew how to audit the books at nice hotels.

But in my heart something was shifting. There was a growing urge to help these people who were destitute and filled with pain. The man on the corner who hadn't eaten in three days. The prostitute who lingered in the doorway of a sleazy run-down hotel.

I knew pain and heartache and hunger too.

For weeks I was in the Tenderloin, walking the dirty streets and praying for whomever would let me, squeezing in time there in the small gaps of my day between work and home. If I could find an extra thirty minutes in my day, I took to the streets. Praying. Watching. Walking with the people. My eyes were opening to a world of despair and brokenness. But it was the children of the Tenderloin who caught me and held me in their grip. What were they doing here with their wide eyes and their shy smiles? Their ragged clothes and dirty fingernails? The Tenderloin was no place for children.... Or was it?

■ ■ ■

The late-afternoon sun hides behind a bank of misty clouds that hover over Turk Street as I step onto the sidewalk with a fistful of tracts in my pocket and my hands full of sandwiches. I make eye contact with an elderly woman who shuffles slowly and steadily toward me with her stockings crinkled around her swollen ankles. An oversize coat engulfs her, and she pushes a handcart full of plastic bags and bottles.

I walk toward her with my hand thrust out, holding a freshly made sandwich. I have always been a loner, withdrawn, holding my thoughts to myself. I am mystified by the change I feel coming over me. It is as if the sight of others' pain and need melts my shyness into a calm purposefulness. I lose my inhibitions in the face of their brokenness.

"Here, take this sandwich." I offer the sandwich to the lady, a hand on her elbow. Her eyes crinkle into a smile as she tucks the sandwich into the front of her basket.

"Thank you."

"God bless you."

Before I can ask if she would like me to pray with her, a commotion catches my eye on the corner of Eddy Street. A small pack of kids is running up the sidewalk at full speed. Racing past storefronts and a shoddy liquor store, their shouts catch in the wind. I say good-bye to the woman and take off after them. *Where are they going?*

I weave in and out of the straggling foot traffic on the sidewalk and break into an easy jog. They are about five hundred feet off. Their laughter hangs in the misty air as I race to catch up. And then they are gone. A giant green building looms up ahead to my right, and I see the door closing behind the last of the children. I slow to a stop in front of the building. I look up, taking in the tiny windows on each floor, the cracks in the faded green concrete, and the rusted fire escapes that trail down the sides of the building. The door is shut.

Gripping the handle, I swing the door open and step into a cramped, dark lobby. Dimly lit sconces hug the walls. The scents of fish and old cooking oil linger in the air. There is no one there. It is as if the shouting children are a figment of my imagination, vanishing at the sound of my steps into their building.

The claustrophobic lobby branches into a tunnel-like hallway pockmarked by a string of dark doors down either side. *Where are they? This is crazy!*

I gingerly knock on the first door. No answer. I try the next door. I hear chatter inside. The door cracks open. Through the opening slit, I see a child. I bend down to his eye level. "Hi!"

Nothing.

"My name is Roger. What is your name?"

Still nothing.

"I'm just here in your neighborhood passing out sandwiches and praying for people. Can I pray for you?"

The door cracks open a little wider, revealing a boxlike room with two beds pressed against each other near the far corner. A pile of clothes covers the end of one bed. A low table with mismatched chairs is shoved against the wall. The boy's bright brown eyes look me over.

Behind his shoulder, I see his playmate, a girl of six or seven, her thick, dark hair braided in a long rope down her back.

"Where is your mom? Is your mom here? Can I pray for her, too?"

The little boy shakes his head. He can't be more than five.

The girl presses herself close to her little brother, answering. "Our mom is at work. We take care of ourselves."

I hear another door open behind me. Looking over my shoulder, I see another pair of dark heads peek out. Two small girls. I try to place their nationality. Cambodian? Thai?

In a creeping realization, the truth hits me. These apartments are not just full of strung-out junkies and prostitutes—although I am sure they live here too. These tiny studio apartments are housing entire families. There are moms and dads and children piled into these dark and damp apartments.

An even crazier thought occurs to me. These kids are here by themselves. Alone. There is no supervision for these little ones. There are no adults in these rooms. The smell of food cooking is not drifting from their apartments. No one is checking in on them or playing with them. They are on their own.

Why aren't they in school? What are they doing alone? Who is protecting them? I could be anyone stepping off of the streets into their home. Some crazy person or child molester.

My heart begins to thump a little harder as my thoughts turn to the types of people who have access to these kids. These little ones are like lambs in a den of wolves. Who knew who was trying to get their claws into them?

"Are you hungry?"

The girl shrugs, her braid dancing with the movement.

The little boy's eyes lock on to mine. A wisp of shiny black hair gets caught on his eyelashes. "Yes."

"And your friends?" I ask, glancing over my shoulder again. The door slams its response. "I'm going to go get you some sandwiches. I'll be back. God bless you."

The boy glances up at his sister. She gives me a nod, as if okaying the bringing of sandwiches. Their hunger seals our friendship.

Pushing the lobby door open into the cool afternoon air, I leave the musty smells of fish and mildew behind me as I glance at my watch. Twenty minutes before I need to get to my next shift. *I have time.* I start the jog back to my car, a plan already formulating in my mind. I'm not going to miss out on another opportunity to take care of God's little ones.

■ ■ ■

Saturday morning looms bright and sunny, a rarity for downtown San Francisco. The city is alive with the joy of the morning. Cars stream down the streets, headed for the parks and the rippling bay. Cyclists are out, cutting lazy trails down the street. The flower shop on the corner opens its door, and the owner is setting out white buckets of yellow daisies and red roses. Their colors seem to promise a warm spring day ahead.

A black duffel bag thrown over my shoulder, I hustle my family into our van. Marie France and Phil get in the back, and Maite organizes the two little ones in their seats.

"Where are we going?" Maite asks.

"We are going to go get some kids and have a fun lesson and tell them about Jesus."

I throw the duffel bag on the floor and hop in. Maite shuts the door and we are off. Navigating the dense Saturday traffic, I lay out my plan to Maite and the kids: "We'll go into the buildings and see if any of the kids want to play with us. We'll invite them to join in with our games, and then we'll have a story about Jesus. Then we'll pass out sandwiches." Glancing at Maite, I see her nodding.

"Do you think their parents will let them come?" she asks.

I hesitate. "I don't know if their parents will actually be there. When I was in the building, I didn't see any adults."

"None?" I hear the concern in her voice.

"I know. It's crazy. But when I went in there this week, the kids were just by themselves in that tiny apartment. I think they will come with us. They are all alone."

I am right. Knocking on one door after the next, children answer without a parent or adult in sight. Others don't even bother to ask the adults who are there. After an invitation of sandwiches and playing games, we have a group of a dozen children in tow. Maite and I start up the street in search of a place to play.

The Tenderloin is a sorry playground for children. The gated park is full of gangsters with menacing stares, and the alleyways between the streets are no better. There isn't a patch of grass in sight or a safe place for a child to catch a ball or run or let their laughter carry them away.

We settle on the Cadillac Hotel, a run-down affair with a battered front lobby and cracking plaster on the walls. Mismatched chairs line the walls and some equally mismatched tenants lounge in them smoking cigarettes and looking at the day's paper.

I've heard there is a generous man there who runs a homeless shelter out of this hotel but I don't see him around. Traces of the Cadillac's former glory are apparent as we find our way to the ballroom. It is a wide space with a high ceiling bordered by an elaborate molding that is weathered and peeling. The glory ends there. There is no electricity and the only light coming in sifts through a few skylights in the ceiling. The kids settle themselves on the floor, waiting expectantly for the fun and food promised. I unzip my bag and hold up a whiffle ball and bat and pull out a ream of used computer paper I found abandoned at the office. "Who likes baseball?"

The kids respond with shouts and waving hands.

"All right! Let's play!"

Marie France and Phil mark out the bases with duct tape, and Maite keeps score on the old paper. The echoing ballroom is filled with the sound of running feet and laughter. Runs are cheered and outs are booed. Michelle and Christian run among the kids as they round the makeshift bases. There are protests as the game comes to an end.

"Okay, everyone. Sit down! Kids, pass out the sandwiches." The thought of food settles them down immediately. Maite holds Christian and caresses the silky head of a small girl who has found her way under her arm. Another boy latches on to Phil and plops down next to him, mimicking his crossed legs and folded arms. Marie France passes out a sandwich to each child.

"I want to tell you today about why we are here. We are here because Jesus loves you very much. More than anyone. Today I am going to tell you a story about who He is and what He did for you."

Several children fidget with the wrappers of their sandwich. One little boy lays his head in the lap of his older sister. She pats his back as she gazes up at the dust filtering through the air, caught in the brightness of the skylights. Two boys in the back mess with each other, flicking each other's ears and batting at each other's hands.

They are a hodgepodge of kids dressed in hand-me-downs and old tennis shoes, but I feel the pull of them and who they are. I see their need as they look around for more sandwiches. I feel their fear and their want like it is my own. I know that Jesus is the only thing that can shift their lives. He is the only thing that has shifted mine.

Finishing my story of Jesus dying on the cross for them, I pray over them: "Oh, God, bless these kids! Help them to know You. Take care of them and protect them! We love You. Amen!

"Okay, kids! Next week we will be back with more food and more games! Do you want to come play again?"

Their boisterous affirmation fills the ballroom.

"Okay! Have a great week and we will see you next week!"

Super Saturday has been born.

■ ■ ■

The next Saturday we are back. As we enter the building to begin gathering the kids up, we are surprised that our small crew has grown. There are twenty children milling around in the lobby. Word has spread of our fun—or at least of our sandwich-making ability.

"Are we playing baseball?" one of the kids calls out.

"Where is the food?" calls another.

I grin at Maite. "They remember us!"

"I hope you brought enough sandwiches."

"Me, too," I whisper under my breath. I have no clue what I am doing, but I have never felt so alive. The excitement of connecting with these kids stretches my face into a grin.

"Okay, everyone! Let's go check out the Cadillac Hotel!"

No one really cares who uses the ballroom. It's a down-and-out place, and the door is always wide open. There is no electricity or water, just a big, empty room.

We push out the door in a crazy mess of large and small bodies.

"Stay in a line, everyone! Don't let the little guys fall behind."

Passersby watch in interest as we make our way toward the run-down hotel. We are a sight. A bright patch in a dark place.

As we head up the street, I start thinking about how we can invite more kids … and maybe some of our church friends to help minister to these little ones. Those dark apartments are filled with a sense of hopelessness. The more kids we can get to join us on Saturday, the better.

■ ■ ■

All I can hope is that we can keep these kids from the darkness that presses in on them on a daily basis. I have begun to pray while I am at work. As I crunch numbers, I am remembering faces and names and reminding God of these little ones who are asking Him for guidance and protection. They are growing on me even after two short weeks.

A couple of months later, we are beginning to develop a routine for our Super Saturday program. Bible stories. Games. Snacks. Laughter. Food. Hope. A few friends from church, as well as from the Chinese Christian Center, are joining us on Saturdays to help care for the kids. We meet for prayer at our house and then head down to the Tenderloin. Our friends are gripped by the needs of the children like we are. They can't believe the hardship, the neglect, the poverty that is within minutes of their own doorsteps. We are all motivated to help.

Miraculously, Dave, a Christian businessman I met, is renting a storefront on Jones Street under the Bel Air Hotel and is letting us meet there on Saturdays. We are partnering with a group of Asian women there who had already started an after-school program. We have started a fledgling youth group and a prayer meeting on Friday nights. We have also begun to take the kids on field trips around the city.

This Saturday we are at the beach. I stop the van and Maite hops out. Opening the doors of the van, the kids spill out like crazy clowns piling out of a circus car.

"Twelve, thirteen, fourteen, fifteen …"

"What are you doing?"

"Seventeen," Maite finishes. "We packed seventeen kids in that car!"

Her laughter is contagious.

The car next to us empties another half dozen children onto the waiting beach.

The pounding of the surf and the cool sand have an invigorating effect on them. They are immediately in the sand, burying each other, running toward the waves, yelling at each other with joy written across their faces.

I grab Maite's hand. "I love this!"

"I know, Roger. I do too!"

Our own kids mingle with the kids from the Tenderloin. They have taken our new Saturdays in stride, as if everyone's family hangs out in one of the poorest sections of San Francisco for fun.

"What are we going to do about tomorrow?" one of the kids asks me.

I raise my eyebrows and rub my hand over my forehead. The last few Sundays, we have taken our new friends to church with us, unloading thirty-five children into our small-town church's Sunday school program. Thirty-five unruly, wild, unchurched children. The effect was nothing short of disastrous. While some of our church friends were prepared to go minister in the Tenderloin, they were not ready for the Tenderloin to come to them.

"Those teachers were not happy with us," Maite reminds me.

"No, they weren't," I agree. "I think we may need to forget taking them to church … at least for now."

Maite nods in agreement and then starts laughing, pressing a hand to her mouth. "I guess they weren't ready for cussing in Sunday school."

I laugh with her and shrug. "They don't know any different, Maite. These kids are survivors. And they are just learning about Jesus. It will take time."

Maite squeezes my hand. "I know."

We follow the kids down to the water. Their joy is contagious. I run after them, splashing and yelling.

Somehow, bringing them here, getting them out of the darkness of the inner city, easing some of their pain, sets me free inside. Bringing light to the heart of a child heals something in my soul. I could do this forever.

■ ■ ■

Super Saturdays become the cornerstone of our fledgling ministry in the Tenderloin even though we are flying by the seat of our pants. I'm amazed at what we get away with shuttling kids across the city. There are no permission slips or parent helpers, and we don't count seat belts. We just cram as many kids as we can into the cars we have. We don't want anyone to miss out. It is hard to believe the influence and freedom we have to intervene in these children's lives.

But just as we are making inroads into the family communities of the Tenderloin, a new type of struggle arises. One I never saw coming.

Before I know it, I will be fighting to keep myself in the Tenderloin, doubting myself, doubting God's call on my life, doubting my ability to lead. Darkness comes in different forms. This is just the first fight to stay … and it will be the first of many.

Chapter 9

FINDING OUR PLACE
IN THE TENDERLOIN

Tenderloin, 1985
Road map

Standing in front of the Bel Air Hotel in the middle of the Tenderloin, I rub my hand against the streaked storefront window. The room is tiny and dark, and the door is locked. Our friend Dave, who has been renting this space for us, has left the city for a job promotion on the East Coast and is no longer covering the cost of the space. The group of Asian ladies whom I partnered with in our after-school program is gone.

My hand pressing against the window, I peer inside. This is our place. The kids are learning about Jesus here. More kids come every week for food and fun and hope. I have paced this concrete floor night after night, praying through the yelling and screaming I hear in the surrounding apartments. We have been bringing light and pushing back darkness here. We have been meeting here for over a year, and now it is gone. *What are we going to do?*

I blow out a long breath and lean up against the cool window frame. I see a few men across the street slip through a darkened doorway to watch a strip show. Steam rises from the street grate near the cocktail lounge next door. I can hear the clinking of glass and laughter roll through the open door as another customer walks inside. A patrol car slowly cases the street. The drug dealers are out in force.

How do I keep these kids safe from all this? You are going to have to do it, Lord. You can do it. You are the only one who can do it.

Leaning up against the darkened window, I close my eyes, thinking back to a few months ago. The memory is as clear as if it happened yesterday.

While walking down the street to meet up with a few of our Super Saturday kids, I saw a middle-aged man with a dirty, striped shirt and a cigarette hanging from his lips talking with two young boys. He leaned down, taking the cigarette from his mouth, and slowly rubbed the shoulder of a skinny boy with a brown mass of haystack hair. I saw him nod his head toward the open door of his apartment building. Immediately a sour taste filled my mouth and my stomach began churning, fueled by a surge of uncontrollable anger.

I yelled out, "Hey! Get away from those kids!"

The man jerked his hand away from the boy's shoulder as if burned. He looked up and down the street to see if anyone else was looking. "What's your problem, man?"

"You are my problem. You stay away from those kids. Don't look at them. Don't talk to them. Don't touch them."

A leer crossed his face. "I'm not doing anything. We're just having a friendly chat."

I closed the gap between us and pulled the kids out of his grasp and closer to me. "Kids, don't talk to this guy. He is no good. Go home."

The boys looked up at the man one last time and, with a push from my hands, took off running up the street.

A string of curses rolled from the man's lips, his eyes flashed with anger as he took a drag on his cigarette and blew the smoke at me, but I was not afraid.

"Listen," I said, pointing my finger at his chest. "I know who you are and what you do to kids. You touch one of those kids again, and God is going to get you."

He laughed. "You're a freak. You don't know what you're talking about."

I took a step closer to him, smelling the ripeness of his unwashed body. "Listen to what I say. Stay away from those kids."

"Whatever." He turned away from me and headed into his building.

A few weeks later I was back on that same street corner, and I saw one of the little boys the man had been talking to. Calling him over to me, I placed both hands on the boy's shoulders and squatted down to chat with him. "Hey, have you been listening to me? You've been staying away from that man in this building, right?" I was smiling but my tone was serious.

He shrugged at me. "He's gone."

"What do you mean he's gone? Did he move?"

He squinted up at me. "Nope. My mom said he died."

My hands dropped from his shoulders, and I stood up in a daze as the boy took off up the street. I was speechless. Shaking my head in disbelief, I turned around and walked the other way. *He died?* Maite was not going to believe this. I couldn't believe it myself.

The memory fades, and I find myself still leaning against our old building, wishing we still had this small room to use for our ministry. Anxious thoughts crowd my mind. *How are we going to keep helping these kids without a building? How can God grow our ministry when it seems like we are meeting opposition at every turn?*

I push off the wall and start walking back to work. For lack of a better choice, we have taken up residence in the old Cadillac Hotel ballroom again. It is a poor substitute for our own meeting place. The absence of electricity and running water puts a damper on our time with the kids. Last week, I suggested we explore the basement for fun, and three of the kids ended up crying due to fear. Not my best idea, but I am running out of good ones.

In spite of it all, Maite continues to amaze me with her energy and hope for the kids in the Tenderloin. She works full-time selling insurance and still shoulders the care of our four kids, letting me come down to the Tenderloin whenever I can. The needs are overwhelming, and my passion to be here is growing daily. I am thankful for each person who is coming to help us. But that brings up another concern.

I rub a hand across my forehead, taking in another deep breath. *Who knew starting a ministry passing out food could be so full of pitfalls?*

An evangelist and a worship leader from our church have really stepped up with their gifts of speaking and worship, involving themselves every weekend. In fact, they have stepped up so much, I think they may be trying to take over. I'm not sure what to do about this. I am not a preacher. I am not a worship leader. I am a man who has been called to serve in the Tenderloin. To set people free with the truth of Jesus. To fill hungry bellies with free sandwiches and glasses of lemonade.

With each step I take toward Parc 55, I shoot silent prayers heavenward. "God, You have helped me over and over. Help me again. We need a place for these kids to meet and learn about You. I need wisdom in dealing with these helpers. I know Your ways are bigger than mine. We need You now."

With one last glance over my shoulder at the dust-smeared window of our old Super Saturday headquarters, I head back up the street to my office. My lunch break is over. It's back to the grind.

■ ■ ■

The beginning years of our ministry were organic and slow growing. We were fueled by our love for Jesus and our desire to serve. We were excited. We were driven. And we were naive.

Some of our hardest lessons lay before us. We had no idea how to start a ministry when we embarked on this journey with a bag full of sandwiches and a handful of kids, but God was guiding us the whole time. He was faithful. Giving wisdom. Granting mercy. Filling us with grace. And we surely needed it then as we do now.

Chapter 10

HOME BASE

Eddy Street, 1986
The beginning ...

It is a cool Saturday as the morning's fog lingers in the air. We are prepping for another Super Saturday on the sidewalk near the Cadillac Hotel. A steady stream of traffic pushes up the street past the intersection of Jones and Eddy. My family is with me. I laugh as I see Christian tickling one of the helpers who has come along with us this morning. That boy always brings a smile to my face.

The evangelist and the worship leader have a small group clustered around them, laughing, nodding at what they are saying. They have a way of attracting people to them. I see Maite glancing over at them as she walks up to me with Michelle in tow.

"Roger, you need to let them know you are leading this meeting today. The kids are here because of you. We are here because of you. I think they think they are in charge."

I shrug, running my hand over Michelle's shiny hair. "Maite, it is good to have so many people helping. I think it will all work out."

She sighs and squeezes my hand. I love that she is mine. Her beauty still catches me off guard, and I trust her like no one else. This mission in the Tenderloin is cementing our marriage in a new way, merging our new passion for God and each other into a life of service. She knows me better than I know myself. I am not one to put myself forward to lead, but she knows this is not just a project or hobby for me. This is becoming my life. I feel the needs of these kids like they are my own. My auditing jobs are becoming less of a career path and more of a means to support my Tenderloin habit. Any moment I can sneak away, I am climbing the stairs in the old buildings, knocking on locked doors, and meeting with people. My first encounter with a family in the green building on Eddy is still emblazoned in my mind like it was yesterday.

■ ■ ■

I knock once, and then twice, as the dim overhead lighting casts weird shadows on the battered doorframe. The musty smell of old carpet fills the hallway. The door opens, and I am amazed to see a large Cambodian family of eight seated around a small table on the floor. The spicy scent of dinner cooking wafts toward me.

"Hi, my name is Roger."

"Yes." The woman who answered the door places a firm hand on the door. A billowing floral dress hangs on her slight frame. With tiny threads of silver lining her black hair, I can't tell her age. Forty? Fifty?

These families of refugees have lived through so much, escaping the war-torn jungles and the brutality of the Khmer Rouge in Cambodia. They looked aged beyond their years by the time they arrived in the United States. They are further traumatized when they realize America is not the haven they thought it would be. Life in the Tenderloin is hard. Living in such small quarters with such a large family on a tiny income must be discouraging.

"I am here passing out sandwiches and praying for people. Would you like me to pray for you?" I motion toward the inside of the apartment.

The woman glances over her shoulder, speaking softly in a language I don't understand. The door opens wider, and she beckons me inside. My heart is racing. I nervously rub my hands together.

"Yes," she says again.

I step inside. The crowded room is only a studio apartment. *How in the world do they all live in here?* A single bed is against the wall and an open rack of clothes stands next to it. Shelving lines the walls. Pots and pans and cooking utensils are shoved next to books and bottles of medicine. A single bulb lights the room, and there is no window to bring extra light.

"Before I pray for you, I would like to share a story with you—a story that has changed my life."

Launching into the story of salvation, I see the family nod their heads. As I speak, I try to place them in my mind. *Grandparents? An aunt and uncle? Cousins? Maybe there is more than one family here.*

I smile at them. "So Jesus came to save us from our sins and set us free. That is the best news of all. Would any of you like to ask Jesus to come into your heart today?"

They all are nodding and smiling at me. A thrill of joy shoots through me. I put a hand on the shoulder of the woman who answered the door to pray for her. She looks confused and moves away from me, so I fold my hands together, praying. "Jesus, these folks would like You to come into their lives. Please forgive their sins and save them today."

They continue to smile and nod as I leave the apartment. My first time to lead an entire family to the Lord! I feel like I am walking on air as I take the steps down to the first floor two at a time.

I found out later that none of them understood a thing I had said, and I had offended the woman by touching her. In American Christian culture, laying hands on someone is a sign of agreeing in prayer with them. In her culture, it is inappropriate behavior from a strange man.

Live and learn. That is what I did every day in the Tenderloin.

■ ■ ■

Maite squeezes my hand again, bringing me back to thoughts of what will take place this morning.

"Roger, I think we are all here!"

"Okay. Great!"

I smile at the friends who are gathered on the sidewalk to help us this morning. This Saturday, we have fifteen volunteers primed and ready to minister to the kids. They are talking together, laughing. Michelle is riding piggyback on one of the youth workers' backs. Marie France and Phil are laughing with a few of the kids from their youth group who have joined us. My heart is pounding out an erratic rhythm in my chest. I rub my sweat-slick palms together. I take a calming breath to steady myself.

We are standing in front of the dusty windows of 302 Eddy Street. An elderly man with a metal cane taps up the street past us and then stops, pausing to listen.

"Listen, everybody! This is the place I was telling you about." Placing my hand on the dirt-encrusted window, I continue. "We need a place to meet with the kids. To have fun with them. We need a place to meet for our youth service and our prayer meeting. I met with the owner of 302 Eddy Street earlier in the week, and he has agreed to rent the storefront for $2,500 a month. The only problem is, we don't have the money to rent it. I want to take a vote to see who is willing to give their tithes toward paying for this building on a monthly basis."

Maite's hand is the first hand to go up. The evangelist and worship leader are smiling and raising their hands. One by one, each volunteer raises their hand. Maite is grinning from ear to ear. So am I.

I clap my hands together and direct the team. "All right then! It's settled! I will sign the lease this week. Now let's go get the kids!"

I feel a closing in my throat and tears prick at the corners of my eyes. Tears of happiness. Tears of joy at a dream being realized.

Three short years ago, I left a boy alone here, hurting on a street corner. Today, on a similar street corner, we are making a place to welcome boys and girls just like him. A safe haven. A place of laughter and learning and hope. For the first time, we will have a building of our own in the Tenderloin.

Walking up the street to head into the building, our resident evangelist catches up to me and matches his stride to mine. I look over at him as he touches my arm.

"Roger, this is perfect! We have been thinking that we should start a church here in the Tenderloin. We'll meet here on Sundays and have the kids come here to the new building."

Caught off guard with my own thoughts of what the building is for, I say nothing.

He continues, "It will be great. We'll have a real presence here in the Tenderloin. God will start to move."

I take a deep breath and stop him with my arm. The rest of the team continues up the street, calling out to kids, ducking into buildings to gather them up for our fun Super Saturday. A pastor friend of mine is coming later to do a karate demonstration. This should get the kids excited.

"I think God is already moving. Kids are coming to know Jesus. I come down here every day and meet with them. I hang out with them in their apartments and talk to their families on my work breaks. We meet on Wednesday nights to pray. We have youth group on Friday nights. Besides, we need to keep supporting our church in Daly City. Don't you think?"

He looks up the street. "Things are changing, Roger. We have momentum. Let's take this thing to the next level." He pats me on the back, not waiting for my response, and jogs to catch up with the rest of the group.

The taste of exhaust fills my mouth as an old car rumbles past me spitting out fumes. Another car honks as a crew of high school students block the crosswalk making rude gestures at the old car.

I look back down Eddy toward the storefront with its darkened windows. There is a lot of work to do. We need to paint and clean and get tables and chairs set up, but this is our next step. A meeting place for our kids to come to. Not a church service.

Maite is coming toward me. "What was that all about?"

"They want to start a church service here."

Irritation furrows her brow. These guys don't realize who they're up against. You don't want to cross the French girl. "Are you kidding? This is not their ministry, Roger." She is facing me and takes my cool hands in her warm ones. "God has called you here … to these kids. You are supposed to lead this."

I lean toward her. "I am leading.… I'm just not sure they are following."

A smile cracks her concerned expression. She lets go of my hand and brushes a strand of hair out of her eyes. "Roger, when we went away to fast and pray last month, we felt like God would give us this building. And look, right here today, all of us agreed it is going to happen. God is with us in this. You keep leading."

I lean in to kiss her cheek. I tell her again, "It will all work out." I say it out loud to ground myself so that I will believe it.

I start back up the street holding her hand. I hope it is true.

■ ■ ■

We are three months into our lease at 302 Eddy Street. Our Super Saturdays are topping out at up to a hundred kids a week. I think of their faces, putting names to them: Maria, Paulo, Ellie, Martin, CeeCee, Laura. Kids from different cultural backgrounds—African-American, Indian, Cambodian, Chinese, Vietnamese, Filipino, Mexican, and Caucasian—all coming together every week to play and learn. All up and down Jones and Eddy, across to Taylor and Turk Street, we go into the buildings and invite them to hear about Jesus, to come play games and laugh with us in this place that so rarely offers laughter.

I am thinking two things: *I love these kids*, and *I am not going to see them again*. Just as it is beginning to take off, it is over.

I am sitting on a metal folding chair across from Maite in the center of our newly leased storefront. Tears are dripping off of her chin and she is angry. She swipes at the tears from her cheeks with both hands. "How can this happen? God put this on *your* heart, Roger! He called *you* here to the Tenderloin. You can't just walk away."

I look out the streaked window. Our evangelist friend and the worship leader have split off from us and launched their own church service directly across the street from us. Our pastor has given them his support and requested that we no longer ask anyone from our church to help us. They have recruited all the workers and kids that I have been working with for the past three years to join them. *My* kids. The ones whom I write letters to and visit and pray over.

"How are we going to pay for this building now? What is going to happen?"

I push back in my chair and send the legs screeching across the cement. "Maite, I don't know. But I know we need to honor the leadership of our church. I don't understand it. I don't know why this is happening this way. It is killing me inside." Tears of frustration roll down my cheeks and drip onto the knees of my pants. "I don't know what God is doing, but I do know that we need to pray."

Maite nods, wiping at her eyes one more time. At least we are in this together.

These are the words that would continually pull at us through-out our time in the Tenderloin. *We need to pray. Now. We need to fast. Today.* We never knew how God would move, but we knew He would, and when He does, it's always in a more powerful way than we could imagine.

God wasn't finished with us. He wasn't finished with the kids we loved so much in the Tenderloin. We knew that in our gut and in the way our hearts bled for the people on the streets. And so the praying began. Hearts in hand, we prayed for God to lead us, for Him to show us His direction and to show us in a real and tangible way that He wanted us to stay in the Tenderloin.

Chapter 11

FINDING OUR WAY

Tenderloin, 1991
God is always faithful.

I lasted all of eight weeks staying out of the Tenderloin. I prayed and fasted for God to give me some direction. He had not changed the desire in my heart to be in the Tenderloin. I couldn't stand being away from the kids. Honoring my pastor and his wishes, I didn't reach out to any of the kids whom I previously was in contact with. I didn't ask any of the friends from church to come help me.

But I knew this. There were more than one hundred kids in that fear-racked corner of the city who needed to hear about Jesus. This is one square mile of pain and heartache. From Van Ness to Powell Street and Market to Post, over five hundred high-rises are packed in here, with almost forty thousand people. Most are living in studio or one-bedroom apartments. Sometimes two entire families are crammed in a one-person space, almost literally living on top of each other. Poverty and homelessness run rampant. Drug addiction is par for the course. A new, violent disease called AIDS is ripping through the community. Prostitution? Gang violence? Hunger? Hopelessness? These daily tragedies mark out the boundaries of this district.

If there is one thing I knew, it was that only Jesus can crack through the depression and despair that fills the run-down buildings and spills out over the street corners. And there were more kids who needed to feel the light of His love pierce their dark world. I couldn't wait one more minute to get back down there again.

We started over from scratch. After two weeks, we were back up to forty kids and growing. In a month, we had one hundred. My heart was so full I could hardly take it in.

A second miracle took place in the weeks following the split. One day, between work shifts, I opened the door to the apartment and bent down to take off my shoes in preparation for a power nap. I looked up and Maite was standing in the middle of the living room, a piece of paper gripped in her hand.

"Roger, you are not going to believe this."

I stepped toward her, apprehensive, but I stopped when I saw the look on her face. Peace. Joy. "What is it?"

"This is a letter from the leasing agent for 302 Eddy. I told her about our situation and the church split. She is lowering our rent by a thousand dollars."

I started to laugh. I couldn't help it. "Are you kidding me?" Lowered rents in San Francisco are unheard of.

"I am not kidding." She joined my laughter.

I grabbed her in a hug, tears stinging the corners of my eyes. Tears of unbelief and happiness. "We should be able to cover the rent with your work and mine. It will be tight, but we can do it."

I breathed in the smell of her, this woman God blessed me with, this woman who is beside me, fighting for me, chasing after God with me.

"I love you," she said.

"I love you, too."

"Now you can take your nap." She laughed again.

For the first time in months, my body relaxed. I couldn't believe it. What God was doing on our behalf was amazing. In the face of such discouragement, God had planted us, despite the odds, on the corner of Eddy and Jones. With this letter came His blessing.

Decades later, the rent stays at that rate. In a city of overblown real-estate prices and staggering rents, God's hand of blessing has enabled us to stake our claim in this patch of the Tenderloin. The years build on each other. The longer we are in the Tenderloin, the more we see the needs. Little ones who need love and guidance. Homeless friends who need a hug and a meal. Addicts who need freedom. Our efforts are a drop in an overwhelming bucket. We need support and bodies to grow the work. This is our constant prayer.

Heal these people, Lord. And send workers to help.

■ ■ ■

I am sitting at a table in the 302 Eddy building. Helen, Connie, Mary, and Angela have left for the afternoon. They are the first four workers we partnered with in our inner-city work. They are tireless in working with the elderly Asian folk in the Tenderloin. Cambodian, Chinese, and English classes keep the seats filled on a daily basis. They warm my heart with their passion to teach and to love. The room is quiet now that they are gone.

A pot of rice is steaming on a hot plate in the back of the room. The scents of soy sauce and simmering chicken and cabbage fill the air. It is pouring outside. The rain runs down the windows in wet sheets, blurring my view of the sidewalk.

I'm getting ready for our Monday-night Bible study. Soon the folding chairs will be filled with residents of the surrounding buildings as they heap their plates with the food I've prepared and open their hearts to the words of Jesus. But for some reason, an emptiness fills me. Even with all we have going on with Super Saturdays, after-school programs, Bible study, Wednesday-night prayer meeting, Friday-night youth group, and Sunday visitations to the buildings.

I lower my head into my hands, my temples throbbing. I am tired. Actually, that is an understatement. I am exhausted. I am surviving on a couple of hours of sleep per night. Why aren't I satisfied? Why is there this empty pit in my gut? *Aren't I doing enough, Lord? I am chasing You with all I have. I am giving You every hour of my day. I am fasting and praying. What do You want from me? Is there something I am missing?*

The rain sputters and then gains momentum, hurtling against the window in a fresh downpour. The lights in the room flicker and then sustain their warming glow. A thought flits through my head: *Are you done with your programs?*

I press my fingertips against my temples. *Programs?*

Another thought pulses through my mind: *If you are done with your programs, I will tell you what to do.*

My shoulders sag under the weight of the question. I put my head down on the table. I am immediately humbled. *What do I need to do, Lord? Tell me. I will do it. You know I will.*

Two actions I have embraced flash across my mind: my constant hand washing, and my reluctance to eat in the homes of the people I minister to. I am pierced to my heart, and I begin to quietly weep. *Forgive me, Lord. All this time I have been longing to minister to these people and bring them the good news of Your love, and yet I have been holding out on them. Not willing to immerse myself in true community. I have been washing my hands of their poverty any chance I can get. Holding myself above them by not eating in their homes. Subconsciously keeping myself out of their reach.*

It is an issue of the heart that God is bringing to my attention.

My thoughts segue to church. We are pouring out our lives here throughout the week, but we are still going to church out of the city. We are keeping ourselves distant from the Tenderloin community in that way too. Despite our differences, we have continued to be a part of the fellowship that we sank our roots into as infant Christians. We have developed close friendships at our church. Our kids are plugged into the youth group there. Our first taste of Christian ministry happened there.

But another thought is planted in my mind. It is time to go. If we want to immerse ourselves in ministry here in the Tenderloin, we need to start a church here. We need to worship with the ones we are ministering to. We need those tender roots that were planted in the soil of our home church to be transplanted to the hungry earth of these impoverished streets.

I wipe at my eyes with the backs of my hands and blow out a deep breath. The emptiness in my gut starts filling with a new sense of purpose. A new path has been laid before me. God is so good in always answering our prayers. Even in ways we don't always expect. Or more like in ways we never expect. I chuckle to myself.

The front door rattles. My first guest has arrived.

"Come on in." I stand with my hand outstretched. No more hand washing for me.

■ ■ ■

This decision shifts the course of our ministry.

Maite is on board with starting our own church even though she cries when we tell our pastor we are leaving. Our pastor and his wife cry too. There is a lot of shared history between us. They have come around in full support of us and our ministry over the years. But I am not sad. I can't be.

There is an opportunity to love the people of the Tenderloin in a new way opening up before us. Humbled, excited, we take one more step toward completely immersing ourselves in the community that already owns our hearts. Now we just need to find a spiritual covering, a denomination to align ourselves with as we head into this next phase of our ministry. We need a group of people to be accountable to and who can support us in the coming days as we grow. The only problem is, we have no idea how to do that.

We do the only thing we can do at this point: we get on our knees and pray.

We are not disappointed. Once again God comes through in a way only He can. He starts by using an eighty-year-old lady with the heart of a lion.

Chapter 12

PRAYING AND FASTING ABOUT WHOM TO WORK WITH

Scotts Valley, 1994
I need covering and protection.

Redwood trees frame the bright-blue sky on either side of the highway as we drop down off of Highway 17 into Scotts Valley. Their majesty and pristine beauty give way to the green valley floor. The upcoming off-ramp has a sign that reads Bethany Bible College.

The drive from San Francisco takes an hour and a half. Just enough time for me to be completely nerve-racked.

I prep Michelle and Christian in the backseat. "Okay, you guys. I want you on your best behavior. These guys are the bigwigs."

"Okay, Dad." They are messing with each other and cracking each other up like teenagers do.

Out of the corner of my eye, I see Maite smile as I downshift. "What are you smiling at?"

"You are going to do great, that is what I am smiling at." She pats my leg.

I wish I felt as confident as she seems. We are on our way to meet with the district officials of our denomination. My latent insecurities are rearing their ugly head. The years of abuse at the hands of my father haunt me in mysterious ways. They have left me unsure of myself when I am in the presence of authority. I would be much more comfortable if Lula Baird were here to walk us through the process.

A year earlier, this firecracker of an elderly woman drove the two hours from Turlock to San Francisco to meet with us. Reverend Lula Baird is a minister and a missionary ordained with the Assemblies of God. Having lived overseas for years, she speaks Chinese fluently. Knowing her soft spot for Asian ministry, I had approached her about our fledgling work in San Francisco, and she graciously decided to take this Chinese immigrant and his French wife under her wing.

Meeting at a Chinese restaurant owned by my friend, the heavenly aroma of the numerous plates that crowded our table surrounded us. I dug into the garlicky prawns and steaming rice as Lula shared some of her history with us.

"Telling people about Jesus is what I love to do. God has put a love for the Chinese people on my heart. There is nothing I won't do to get God's Word to them, but I have also had the support of my fellow ministers as I am working." She took a drink from her water glass and dabbed at her face with her napkin. Her white curly hair framed her face and a determined look set her mouth in a firm line.

"The Assemblies of God needs to take you in and support you. The work you are doing is the work God wants done. The district needs to be behind you."

I had visited with the leaders of different denominations trying to find a good fit for our Tenderloin ministry. We wanted the spiritual covering and support base of a larger group of churches. We had a loose affiliation with the Assemblies of God since our old church was a part of their fellowship. I knew we needed to align ourselves with a denomination and the help they could offer us, but I hadn't known how to go about it.

I am not like other ministers who have gone to Bible college or who have known Jesus for their whole lives. I don't have connections. I don't have the network of friendships that so many people who have careers in ministry have. I don't have the family connections that some ministers have either. There is no generational heritage for me. I am a loner. I've slipped into ministry through the back door, simply following the course that Jesus has laid out for me. Besides, the Assemblies won't ordain someone as a pastor if they or their spouse have been divorced. Maite was divorced before we met and before God turned our lives inside out.

I rubbed my hands together and folded them, looking across the table at Lula. "Okay. That sounds good, but how do we do that?"

The waiter stopped to clear our table and fill our water glasses. Lula's eyes were twinkling as she leaned across, reaching out her vein-lined hands to us. She took our hands in her own. "I am going to make some calls."

A sense of relief welled up in me. I smiled at Maite. This was a woman who had survived two world wars, the planting of forty

Chinese churches, a turbulent missionary life, and who still flew overseas regularly at the age of eighty. She was a force to be reckoned with. I had an overwhelming sense that there were very few people who said no to Lula Baird when she called.

I remind myself of this divine appointment as we pull into the driveway of the district office. It is a low-slung wood building that sits at the base of a long drive that leads up to the district's Bible College campus where Marie France is attending school. I see Marie France standing at the glass doors of the entrance, waiting for us. I squint at her and whisper under my breath, "Maite! Why is Marie France wearing a miniskirt?"

The kids jump out of the backseat and run to hug their big sister. It is strange to see that they look so tall next to her. Before I know it, they will be coming to school here too.

"Roger, relax! Marie France looks beautiful. Everything is going to be fine."

Maite is right. Marie France is beautiful. Her curly brown hair catches the sunlight as she hugs Christian and Michelle. Their laughter reaches us as we step out of the car.

I shrug my shoulders, rolling my head to one side and then the other. I take a long, deep breath, inhaling the woodsy scent of the eucalyptus and pine trees surrounding the building. Grabbing Maite's hand for support, I head into the building, bringing my family with me.

The silver-haired assistant district superintendent, Brother Earl, greets us warmly in the small lobby. "Roger and Maite! Welcome!"

Ushering us into a conference room, the table is surrounded by twelve pastors and district officers. They are chatting with each other, easy in each other's company. Large windows let in the light filtering through the trees outside. My heart kicks in my chest. Maite squeezes my hand.

These are not my people. I am more comfortable eating a bowl of soup with a homeless man or playing a round of kickball with a ten-year-old. I felt easy and calm with Lula Baird, but here, in this place, with these men of power who could influence the course of my ministry, my mouth is dry and light sweat breaks out across my forehead.

Lord, what have You gotten me into? Get me back to the Tenderloin. I'd rather be anyplace but here.

As Pastor Kenny Rogers makes introductions all around, he says, "Roger, we know that you are doing a great thing up in San Francisco. Why don't you tell us your story?"

I take a seat at the table, and Maite and the kids settle in next to me. My voice cracks a little as I begin. Somehow my accent always seems stronger when I am nervous. I watch their faces as I talk about my troubled background, coming to Christ, and my encounter with Jesus after I left the boy in the Tenderloin.

Maite nods sympathetically as I speak. She is always in my corner. The nearness of her grounds me.

It is quiet except for the sound of my voice and the occasional passing car headed up toward the college.

"This is our tenth year in the Tenderloin. We have a building that we meet in all throughout the week for prayer meetings, Bible study, and youth group ..." As I pause to take a breath, one of the elders interrupts me.

"Roger, it seems that God has placed an amazing call on your life and you are following it well. But can you tell us why you are here and what you want from us?"

The others lean forward for my response. His words stop me as if I have hit a wall. In a moment, I am transported in my mind to a memory from three years earlier.

I was leading a prayer and fasting retreat in Albion with a group of men from my church. Sabine, the owner of the camp, gives us free reign of the place whenever we go. Tucked up in a wooded area off the Mendocino Coast, Lord's Land had become a refuge for me. A place of holing up and meeting with God. Groves of windswept trees surrounded the big house and the cabins we were staying in.

We were two days into the retreat and a dark, weighted depression had settled over me. Sending the other men out to walk the grounds and pray, I sat on the edge of the couch in the big house, my head in my hands. Thoughts swam through my mind. *Why do I still struggle to love Maite the way she needs to be loved? Why does hatred for my mom and dad continue to resurface after so many years of prayer? How do I spend time with my kids and still do all that needs to be done for the kids in the Tenderloin?*

I couldn't pray. A groan escaped my lips. *How can I keep working two jobs and continue to lead this ministry whose needs just seem to grow? What do I do with all this stress?*

A Scripture reference surfaced in my thoughts. Galatians 2:6–10. I picked up my Bible from the seat next to me on the couch. A steady breeze caught the limbs of the trees, moving them to beat a steady rhythm against the house. The words lifted from the page as I read them:

> As for those who were held in high esteem—
> whatever they were makes no difference to me; God
> does not show favoritism—they added nothing to

my message. On the contrary, they recognized that I had been entrusted with the task of preaching the gospel to the uncircumcised, just as Peter had been to the circumcised. For God, who was at work in Peter as an apostle to the circumcised, was also at work in me as an apostle to the Gentiles. James, Cephas and John, those esteemed as pillars, gave me and Barnabas the right hand of fellowship when they recognized the grace given to me. They agreed that we should go to the Gentiles, and they to the circumcised. All they asked was that we should continue to remember the poor, the very thing I had been eager to do all along.

"Okay, Lord, what does this scripture mean for me? You know I want to work with the poor just like Paul. I don't know if I am doing it right but I'm doing my best. I don't know how the rest of this passage applies to me."

You will be meeting with the super-apostles, and they will offer you the right hand of fellowship.

I placed the Bible next to me and rested my head against my hands again. The thought went through my mind a second time: *You will be meeting with the super-apostles, and they will offer you the right hand of fellowship.*

"Okay, Lord, I don't understand what this means right now, but I will take it as Your word to me in this moment."

This split-second memory fades from my mind as I face the twelve elders in front of me around the conference table. The fullness of those words three years ago is coming to pass in this moment. I am meeting the super-apostles, and God has given me His word to speak. The fullness of His presence in this moment overwhelms me, and tears begin spilling down my cheeks.

The men are caught off guard, glancing at each other, murmuring.

I ask, "Do you mind if I just read you something from the Scriptures?"

The assistant district superintendent nods. "Go ahead, Roger. We are listening."

I read the passage from Galatians, tears dropping onto the pages of my Bible. Finishing, I look up. My voice breaks as I say, "Brothers, all I am asking for is your right hand of fellowship."

As if the scripture has cracked open their hearts in that moment, the men around the table begin to cry, wiping at their eyes. Our leader stands and says, "Roger, you've got it. You have our right hand of fellowship."

There is a sense of camaraderie that lifts the elders and officials from their chairs. "Let's adjourn this meeting and pray for our brother Roger."

The men, whom I greeted in a state of severe apprehension, gather around me, clapping hands on my back and shoulders, adding their prayers to Earl's as he blesses us. The super-apostles surround me and my family and welcome us, accepting us into their fellowship.

I have no thought that at this moment the groundwork is being laid for one of the biggest miracles to take place in our ministry so far. As I grab Maite in a fierce hug, I have no clue that in a few short months, God will be pushing me out of my comfort zone, launching me into a lifestyle of relying on Him that I have never experienced before. I am merely caught up in the goodness of the moment and the wideness of God's creativity and grace.

Our silver-haired friend places his hands on Christian and Michelle's heads. "We are glad to have you and your family, Roger. I believe that God is going to do great things through you and your ministry in the Tenderloin."

He has no idea that he has just set into motion a chain of events that will play out in front of the entire district. None of us do.

www.sfcityimpact.com

Roger and Maite founded SFCI in 1984.

Annual SF City Impact planning meeting with staff

*Roger and Maite's sixteen grandchildren: Clayton, Gabrielle, Cade,
Abraham, Kahaleana, Cal, Ezra, Malachi, Elle Louise, Isabelle,
Micah, Sophie, Canaan, Maiya, Joelle, and Hunter*

*Marie-France, MZ, and
Michelle serving at SFCI's
annual holiday events*

Enjoying ministry together as a family

Clint and Marie-France

Philip and Rossie

Roger and Maite's children and their spouses

Jody and Michelle

Christian and Cori

Mr. and Mrs. Sun, who gave a bag of gold coins to Roger and Maite for the mission

Prayer intercessions and worshiping in May Chan's home

*Over 5,000 young people come to serve during their spring
and summer break at SF City Impact every year.*

*SFCI's volunteers gather—1,200 in total. Ready to bless the community
and serve over 10,000 meals. P. Roger sharing the vision for the day*

Faithful volunteers:
Lindsey, Ben, Chuck, Leslie, Kristen, Roger, Bill, Christian, Chris and Kevin

Another SFCI event. San Francisco City Impact exists to
intervene on behalf of the Tenderloin Community.

Chapter 13

PRAYING AND FASTING
ABOUT GOING FULL-TIME

San Jose, 1994
Dreams come true.

The church is huge. There is no getting around it. Wide cement pillars hold up the long portico over the entrance. A few cars are parked under it, letting out their elderly passengers. Wide glass doors open into an enormous foyer where hundreds of people are talking, laughing, and waiting to take their seats in the wide auditorium.

This is the place I am supposed to speak. Earlier in the month, I'd had a meeting with our assistant district superintendent. I'd rushed home between auditing shifts for a quick shower and nap before meeting up with him. Dozing off, my mind was caught up in a dream. In the dream, a paraplegic man was placed in my arms. I couldn't move.

Waking up with a start, I'd grabbed my coat and mentioned the dream to Maite as I headed out the door: "I hope this weird dream doesn't have anything to do with my meeting today." It didn't.

Sitting across the table from me at a swank San Francisco hotel, he'd taken a sip from his coffee cup and shared his plan. "Roger, I want you to take a ten-minute window and share your story at the district's upcoming annual business meeting. It will be a way to invite support, financially and spiritually, from other pastors in our area."

I nodded in agreement, toying with the eggs on my plate. "Sure. That sounds great. Thanks for letting me do this."

My wavering smile gave a hint of my inner thoughts: *A ten-minute talk in front of a thousand pastors, ministry leaders, and laypeople? You have got to be kidding me.*

"There will be three of you sharing about your ministries before the keynote speaker comes up. I think it will be great!"

The generous man didn't seem to notice me nervously folding and unfolding my hands as he dug into his fruit cup.

Suddenly I was not so hungry. It seemed that God enjoyed putting me in a place of discomfort and nervousness.

Now the moment has arrived. Here I am, in this enormous church, getting ready to speak in front of all these people I have never met. I feel half paralyzed entering the foyer.

"Maite, I can't do this." I am holding her hand. My hand is wet with sweat.

"Roger, this is one of the ways God can help us. When these people hear about our work in the Tenderloin, they are going to want to be a part of it. I know you are nervous, but you will do great." Her brown eyes flicker over my dark suit, and she brushes an invisible piece of lint off my shoulder. She plucks at the pocket of her stylish new dress with her free hand.

Eyebrows raised, I tell her, "I know you are nervous too."

She breaks into the wide grin I love so much. "I know I am. I feel like I could be sick, Roger. But you are going to do great."

Our laughter eases our nerves.

Moving through the crowd, we make our way to the front of the sanctuary to find our seats. Mammoth curtains hang behind the stage, shaping a backdrop for the choir loft. The platform spans the front of the sanctuary in a wide semicircle. The large overhanging balcony that fills the back of the sanctuary mirrors the shape.

The worship band is setting up for the upcoming service. Piped-in worship music plays softly in the background. The pulpit is dwarfed by the largeness of the entire space. If I could escape I would.

As he sees us come down the center aisle, Earl calls out, "Roger! Great! You are here! Come sit right here, and we'll call you up before the speaker comes on." He motions for me to sit in the front pew and wanders off to talk to one of his pastor friends.

An announcement is made that the service is starting and people begin to take their seats. My breathing quickens, and I rub my palms on my suit pants. I can feel Maite tense up next to me. She is praying under her breath.

I would rather be in the drug-ridden park in the middle of the Tenderloin than here.

A swell of organ music matches the building nausea that is overtaking me. The six days of fasting I did to prepare for this talk only seem to add to my stomach upset. *Why did I ever agree to do this?*

We are two songs into the service when a commotion breaks out near the back of the church. Over the singing, we hear a call for help. "Somebody call an ambulance! I think this man has had a heart attack!"

We crane our necks to see what is going on but can only see a group of people surrounding a man lying on the floor.

The organ music falters. No one knows what to do. Do we stop singing? Do we pray?

Within minutes, the paramedics are there administering CPR and calling for silence: "Please be quiet so we can listen to the heartbeat."

We are suspended in the moment, waiting to see what will happen.

I hope this means I don't have to speak. God, let this mean I don't have to speak.

As they lift him onto the gurney to take him to the ambulance, a well-known pastor leaps to the stage, taking the mic. "Friends, don't you see what is going on here? There are people everywhere who are dying. We need to repent tonight. We need to get right with God. Let's spend some time tonight at the altar."

In that moment, the planned program is forgotten. People surge toward the front of the church. Some are crying. Others are already praying as they make their way down the aisles.

In a moment of recognition, I turn to Maite. "This is it!"

A frown furrows her brow. "This is what?"

"This is the dream! The dream I had last month! The paraplegic man was put in my arms, and I couldn't move. That was God's way of showing me that I wouldn't be speaking tonight! That something was going to happen to stop me."

Maite puts her arm around my shoulders. "Whatever happens, we know that God is in control, right? If you are not supposed to speak, then you won't speak. God will meet our needs some other way."

Relief surges through me. My chest relaxes as I take a deep breath. Despite my concern for the man who has been carried out, I am so glad that I am not going to speak that I can't stop smiling. Bowing my head, I join in with the prayers that are being prayed around me. *Thank You, God, thank You that I don't have to speak. I know You will figure out another way to get us the money we need.*

I was too quick with that prayer of thanks. God works in mysterious and often tricky ways. I should have known this.

■ ■ ■

The next morning finds Maite and me in the back row of the sanctuary at the business meeting. The district officials are seated behind a row of tables that runs across the platform. The secretary/treasurer is reading a portion of Robert's Rules of Order over the microphone. The delegates and voting members of the assembly are chatting. A vote has just concluded, and it is almost time for lunch.

There is a break as they take time to count the ballots. I flick Maite's hair off of her shoulder and poke her in the side playfully.

"Roger, cut it out!"

I am so relieved to have the speaking engagement off my back I poke her again.

She laughs. "Get a hold of yourself."

Putting my arm around her, I squeeze her close.

"Listen to what they're saying."

The hum of background noise fades as I hear my name being called. My stomach lurches. A friend and fellow pastor, Kenny, is holding the microphone. "My friend, Roger Huang, was supposed to speak last night and when everything happened, he didn't get a chance to share about his ministry in the Tenderloin. Why don't we let him share while the votes are being counted?"

In a single moment, the air is sucked out of the room. *Kenny, what in the world are you doing?*

A district official steps up and takes the microphone. "Roger Huang, are you here today?"

I hear myself answer, "I'm here."

Dazed, I feel Maite push me forward, and I make my way to the front. *How is this happening?*

I walk up the side stairs to the front of the platform and stand next to Earl, who introduces me.

"Now a lot of you don't know Roger, but he started a ministry in the Tenderloin ten years ago all the while working two jobs. Why don't you tell everyone about your story, Roger?"

Clearing my throat, I look out over the audience. Hundreds of pastors and their church delegates are waiting to hear what I have to say. "I am not anyone special. I'm just a Chinese immigrant who was found by God."

The story slips from me with ease, as if I am talking with friends. As I talk, my nerves calm. I see the crowd responding to me, listening about the boy in the Tenderloin, about our Super Saturdays and the children we are bringing hope to.

I look out toward Maite and see her nodding as I talk. She knows the truth of our story. She has lived it with me.

"This is our tenth year in the Tenderloin, and really, we just want to do more, tell more people about Jesus, meet their physical and spiritual needs. We just want to serve the poor. Thanks for listening to my story this morning."

Applause breaks out across the auditorium as I hand the microphone back to Earl.

A woman stands up near the front. "I am a missionary in Africa. Where I come from, when we hear a testimony like that, we take an offering."

"Well, this is District Council, and we're still counting votes, so we are not going to do that today," the voice of our superintendent rings out from the table behind me.

I nod and smile and start to make my way off the platform, but Earl stops me. The missionary is coming toward us. The front of the platform is head high for her, and she reaches into her purse and then up to the platform and lays a pile of bills near my feet.

My throat tightens as I look up and see another pastor, and then another, follow her lead and make their way down the aisle. One after the other, each person who comes lays a check or a handful of cash in a growing pile on the platform. Earl can't stop grinning, and I hear a chuckle as the general superintendent stands up from the table and comes around to us.

"Well, brothers, it looks like we better get behind this, doesn't it?"

More applause echoes throughout the building.

Turning to me, as the money pile continues to grow, he asks, "Roger, how much would it take for you to be able to quit your jobs and do ministry in the Tenderloin full-time?"

I hesitate. "About two thousand dollars a month."

"Okay, folks. Our church could do this by itself, but I want to give you a chance to get blessed. Write out your monthly pledge of support for the Tenderloin ministry and pass them to the center of the aisle. Let's get Roger doing what he should be doing."

My breath is catching in jerks. God has just pulled the rug out from under me. He is overwhelming me once again with His creativity and provision.

I clasp hands with our district leader. "Thank you. Thank you."

He grips my hand and smiles at me.

That grip solidifies a friendship that continues on for years. Capital Christian Center still supports us to this day. And the tally for the monthly pledges came in at eighteen hundred dollars. That support has been a constant throughout our ministry.

It seems that God is not through surprising us though. The miracles are just beginning.

Chapter 14

PRAYING AND FASTING FOR 230 JONES STREET

San Francisco, 1997
Gold coins and cash come from a remote source.

The room is dark as sheets of rain run down the windows. The sun has yet to rise, but it's doubtful it will show itself at all today, as the black clouds form a dark curtain in the sky. Sounds on the usually busy street below are muted. Hopefully, our homeless friends who normally wander the streets under my window have found shelter. The room is bare except for a folding table surrounded by chairs that is in the middle of the room. My office. My prayer room. No one visits me here.

I pace the perimeter of the room, calling out into the dim space. "God, do You hear me? I believe You showed me this building. I know You did. Coming to this place was not a mistake. But You have to help us. We can't do this on our own. We are desperate. We don't have the money."

The clatter of raindrops is deafening in the silence.

"What do You want me to do?"

The Bible lies silent on the table.

I am on my fourth time reading it through. Nothing jumps out. Nothing is speaking to me.

Next to my Bible is the letter that has me pacing the floor. I am utterly alone in this building. Not even the transients trying to catch a nap or the druggies I occasionally find shooting up in the halls are here. It seems like a lifetime ago that I spotted the sign outside this building. It happened three years ago on a day when the sun couldn't get any brighter.

■ ■ ■

Standing at the corner of Jones and Eddy, I see a sign inside the dirt-streaked window of the old Musicians Union building at 230 Jones Street. Interested, I make my way down the street, passing the liquor store and sex club that butt up against it. A locked iron gate encloses the entrance and its small alcove.

I peer in the storefront window next to the gate, hands shading my face to keep back the sunlight. The room is rough. Dingy paint covers the walls, and it is easy to see where slipshod repairs have been made to holes in the drywall. There are random groupings of chairs and tables. Scattered papers fan out across a folding table. An ancient light fixture hangs limply from the ceiling.

Biting my lip, I feel a quickening of my pulse. *This is it. This is the answer to our prayers.* We need a new building for our center. Our small space at 302 Eddy can't accommodate all the programs we are running. We are packed in there like sardines.

I step back on the sidewalk and glance up. Three full floors. Three enormous floors for Super Saturdays, for our prayer time, for offices. My thoughts spin off in a thousand directions. *We could feed people here. There is room for a full kitchen. The church could meet here.*

Taking down the number on the sign, I head back over to our center to call around and see what I can find out.

After meeting with the president of the Musicians Union, I sit down with the agent representing the sale to write an offer. He meets me at 302 Eddy.

Looking like a member of the Rat Pack, his slick suit and skinny tie seem out of place with our mismatched chairs and duct-taped table. Art projects from our after-school program and cardboard posters announcing upcoming events line the walls. The smell of coffee brewing in the pot mingles with the exhaust fumes coming in off the street. This is the lull in the day before we begin serving up hot meals to the regulars in our homeless ministry.

Seated across the table from him, I lean forward in my chair, barely containing my excitement. "This building is going to be perfect. Really perfect for what we want to do here."

The agent smiles, nodding, and pulls out a legal pad on which to jot down notes. "That is terrific, Roger. I understand that you want me to write up your offer for the building and represent you as a buyer for the sale."

"Yes!"

"Okay. And you want to offer the full 1.2 million dollars that we are asking for?"

"Yes."

"Okay, great! Now I'll need your tax returns for your income information and where you are going to get your loan from …"

"Well, Maite and I quit our jobs this past year to go full-time in the ministry. So, really, our income is what comes into the Good News Tenderloin Center through donations."

He stops writing and just stares at me. "And what is that income?"

I pause. "Well, at least a couple thousand a month. Of course, a lot of that goes toward feeding the homeless and the rent here, but I'm sure we can work something out."

He is still not writing. I am hearing Maite's voice in my head as I see the look of concern that is etched across his face: *"Roger, only two thousand? We make more than two thousand. Why didn't you say four thousand when they asked you how much support we needed to go into full-time ministry?"* She is right, as usual. San Francisco is not a cheap place to live. Renting 302 Eddy alone is fifteen hundred a month. That doesn't even include renting our own home.

"Look," I say, placing my hand on the desk. "I know it seems crazy. But if you write this offer, the money will come. Most weeks we are praying for our food. And He always comes through just in time. We have enough for us, for the kids we are working for. We have enough for the homeless ministry. We don't know how it happens, but God does it every time. We will start looking for funding. Just write the offer."

Shaking his head, he puts his pen down and rubs his chin with his hand. Moments tick by.

God, please help him help us. I am shooting prayers at the ceiling.

Lifting his chin and looking directly into my eyes, he nods. "Okay, Roger. I don't understand how you are going to do it, but I'll write the offer."

I let out the breath I have been holding in. "Thank you so much," I say, standing and shaking his hand. "Let me know what you need from me and I'll get it for you. Thank you for representing us in this."

He is still shaking his head as he heads out the door.

I follow him out, and as he turns toward the parking garage, I head across the street to 301 Eddy, where Maite is working in our new thrift store. I can't help staring across at 230 Jones as I cross the intersection. I love that building already.

With one last glance at the building, I push open the door for the cheery thrift store. Lined with cast-off racks from a department store and filled to capacity with donated clothes and housewares, the store is open to the community, offering them clothes at a fraction of the cost a regular store would charge. The pastor and his wife from our old home church have outdone themselves helping us stock the shelves.

Maite is arranging some bowls and water glasses that were recently donated. She turns at the sound of the door. "Well? How did it go?" Her look is hopeful.

I break into a grin. "He wrote up the offer."

She starts laughing and I join her. We both know how crazy, how impossible this dream is.

Okay, God. Now it's up to You.

■ ■ ■

A few months after I spotted the For Sale sign in the window, a flashy Mercedes pulls up outside our building. The presence of such glitz on Eddy Street causes a stir. Kids stop their activities and crafts and peer out the window to get a better look.

"Keep working on your homework, guys," I say as I look out the window myself.

Ralph, who has recently joined us full-time in the Tenderloin, moves to take my place at the table where I am sitting next to a young Indian girl working on her homework. His support of our work and his coming are gifts to us. He smiles at the girl, showing her how to work the math problem.

Smiling to myself, I push open the door as a large African-American gentleman in a flashy suit steps out of the Mercedes. The sun glints off the large golden cross he is wearing as he steps up on the sidewalk.

"Brother Huang?"

"Yes?" I hold out my hand to shake his. He grips my hand firmly, introducing himself as the pastor of a large inner-city church across the bay in Oakland.

"I've heard about you and your ministry from across the bay in Oakland. I heard you want to buy a building."

"Yes, we're praying that God is going to give us the finances to pay for that building," I answer, pointing across the street toward 230 Jones. I take in his car and his nice clothes. *Maybe he is the answer to our prayer. Maybe God has sent him to help us.*

Wrinkling his forehead and fixing me with a stare, he says, "Well, I have a word for you, Brother Huang. If you want that building, you need to rent a room in there and start praying for God to give it to you." He continues his pensive stare.

"Okay, Pastor," I answer, a little deflated. "Thanks for taking time to come and tell me that."

He pats me on the shoulder, gets back in his car, and takes off. Shaking my head, I go back inside.

A week later I rent a room in the Musicians Union building. My office. My upper room. The place where I pace and pray and weep and ask God to intervene on our behalf.

A year after writing the offer, I also rent the second floor to use as a meeting room for our church. Another business, an adult day center, has moved in on the ground floor, but inch by inch, we are filling this building with the work God has put on our hearts: feeding people, turning their souls toward God; loving the kids who don't get enough love at home; and speaking the light of truth into this dark corner of San Francisco.

Our place at 302 Eddy is not big enough to contain the needs that swarm around us on a daily basis. Each group of church volunteers that comes to help with our work is asked to lay hands on the 230 Jones building to pray, believing God will give it to us.

Lula Baird comes from Turlock and climbs the stairs from basement to roof. With each faltering step and Maite holding her up, she prays that God will give us this building.

Sometimes God takes years to answer my prayers. I know this in my gut. I know God does things in His own timing. I can be patient. At least I think I can.

■ ■ ■

Picking up the letter off of the table, I scan it again. Another offer has been placed on 230 Jones. We have three months to come up with our down payment or the other offer will be accepted. A feeling of despair rises in me. I have had the letter on this table for a month. The clock is ticking.

Hands placed on the back of my head, I circle the room. I have worn a path in the floorboards this past month. If the drab walls of this room could talk, they would tell stories of my wishes, my hopes, my dreams, which are spoken out loud and fill the stale air daily. They would speak of the inner battles I wage against insecurity, anger toward my parents, and a jealousy for my wife's attention even when I am so busy I can't think—the lack of affection and the deep cruelty I experienced in my childhood seems to create an insatiable need for love in me, a vacuum in my soul. And then these walls would speak of the darkness and the depression that haunt me when I fast. The loneliness and sense of grief that come when I pray for the impossible.

I wish there were some other way to conquer the problems I face. But the growing challenges of the ministry and my deep personal struggles can only be conquered when I lay myself out before this loving God I am chasing and wait on Him. I drop to the floor, laying myself out on the carpet. The tears come slowly, and then in a steady outpouring, mirroring the torrential rain outside.

God, what are You going to do about this building?

■ ■ ■

I call everyone I can think of. Everyone who has shown an interest in our ministry or given in the past. Anyone who comes to mind who can help us make this dream come to pass. I even call the leader of our entire denomination. Nothing.

I feel like I have hit a brick wall. I blow out a huge breath and open the door of the office. Maite has been praying while I have been calling. She is sitting, eyes closed, lips moving. She glances up at the sound of the door opening. "Well? Anything?"

I shake my head.

Maite's eyebrows raise, a look of determination setting her mouth in a line. "Roger, are you ready?"

"Ready for what?"

She stands up and walks over to me, taking my face in her hands. "You know what. We need to fast."

I wrap my arms around her and pull her close as the tears come. Her curly hair brushes my face.

"Okay," I breathe into her shoulder. "Let's do it. Forty days. For this building."

People think that I am spiritual because I fast. I've said it a million times. I will say it again. I fast because I am desperate. Because there is no way out. Because the impossible is blocking my path. Because I will do whatever I have to do to get God's attention. And He is faithful each and every time and meets me in my state of desperation.

People expect me to walk around on some holy high when I fast, as if my lack of food gives me a spiritual bubble of grace to reside in. It is the exact opposite.

Fasting lowers all my defenses. As each day passes, I am gripped by the futility of the world around me. Joy is stripped from my frame. And my stomach hurts. A lot.

■ ■ ■

Sucking down sips of lukewarm coffee, trying to ease the nausea, I look over at Maite.

Kids of every size and color are hard at work in our center, crowded around the tables. The room is filled with their chatter. Backpacks are stacked against the wall near the door. School has just gotten out. Our volunteers are here to help with homework. Pencils and crayons are strewn across the tables as the kids get to work.

Sitting at one of the homework tables in the center, Maite has a little girl on her lap and is stroking her dark wavy hair. "Jesus loves you. You know that, right?"

The little one responds by snuggling into her arms.

The olive tone of Maite's skin is a little drawn, a little pale. But her smile is the same. Always.

"Thirty-one days." She is a mind reader.

"Thirty-one days," I answer her.

Squeezing Katie tight, she says, "Roger, no matter what happens. We have been faithful. Faithful to what God has called us to do."

I nod. She is right.

Putting my cup down, I hop off of the table I am sitting on and walk over to her, placing a kiss on the top of her head. The sounds of the street interrupt us as the door to the center swings open.

Looking up, I see an elderly Chinese woman let herself in. Her cabled, pink sweater dwarfs her, reaching almost to her knees. Her eyes fold into a smile, spotting me.

"Pastor Huang?" She beckons me. I have never seen her before in my life.

"Yes?" I move toward her.

She grasps both my hands. "I have been praying for you. We have been praying for you. God bless you in your ministry."

As quickly as she came in, she turns to go and is back out the door, leaving a slip of paper in my hands. A check. I open it. It says $5,000. Five thousand dollars is in my hand.

"Maite, five thousand dollars! She just gave me a check!"

Maite stands, setting the girl down, mouth open, speechless.

Grabbing the door, I swing it open. The woman is already halfway up the street. "Thank you! Thank you!" I yell after her.

Without turning she raises her hand in a wave. Standing in the doorway, I turn to Maite. "What just happened?"

She is laughing uncontrollably. I see a tear slip down her cheek.

The miracle is beginning.

All week long there is a steady stream of elderly Asian folk who stop by to drop off checks. One thousand. Four thousand. Seventeen thousand. We don't know what to do with ourselves. It is as if the floodgates have opened.

One of the ladies offers us an invitation: "Please come to this address this Wednesday at noon. We have a prayer meeting, and we would like to pray for you."

"Of course! We will be there!"

Driving up Jones Street, we leave the darkness of the Tenderloin behind us and make our way toward Nob Hill. It's hard to believe that the street that threads itself through the Tenderloin is this same street lined with mansions and beautifully groomed lawns.

We arrive at the house. Green oaks outline the steps that lead up to the three-story Victorian. A breeze off of the bay sweeps across the porch as we ring the bell. The owner welcomes us warmly. "Pastor Roger! Maite. Come in."

Immediately we are surrounded by the sound of voices lifted in singing Cantonese hymns to God. Turning out of the entryway, we enter a grand living room crowded with around forty elderly Asian worshippers. Wide windows let in the brightness of the afternoon and offer a view of the windswept bay and its bridges. I recognize several of the faces from their recent trips to our center to drop off their offerings.

"Pastor Roger." The leader of the group, May, a posh woman with sleek gray hair, beckons me to the center of a semicircle of chairs. "We are so glad you are here. Welcome to my home. We wanted you to come here so that we could pray for you." The love that is emanating from this room is tangible. "You should know that we have all been meeting for the past thirty years praying. One of the things we have been praying for is that God would send someone to minister in the Tenderloin." Having me kneel at the center of the room, she says, "We believe that someone is you. You are the answer to our prayer." A sense of overwhelming peace fills the room as she places her hands on my shoulders. "Let's pray for Pastor Roger."

A chorus of forty voices rings out into the arced ceiling, calling on the God who hears our every hope and prayer. Tears slip down my cheeks. Overwhelming tears of gratefulness and hope. God is on the move.

How does a lonely immigrant boy come to find himself in a rich house on Nob Hill being spoken over by a group of prayer warriors? Because of a great miraculous God who does not stop chasing after us. Because of a creative God with a great sense of humor. Because of a loving Father God who meets His children in the moment of their greatest need with His perfect provision. I am continually amazed by His creativity.

While we are visiting after the prayer time, several more checks are pressed into our hands.

As we are leaving the meeting, hugging these dear people, an older gentleman, face wrinkled into a smile, stops me with his arm. "I would like you to come to my house this week."

There is a calmness and steadiness to his voice that I respond to. "Of course, let me know when."

Maite and I get into our car in a state of holy shock, laughing and crying. *What is God going to do next?*

Two days later we are climbing the stairs of another large, beautiful home and ringing the doorbell. The ornate oak door opens, and a small Chinese woman with gray, bobbed hair and a lovely smile lights up at the sight of us. "Come in, come in!"

She leads us into a front room, which is lined with filing cabinets and a grouping of chairs. Her husband is sitting in one of the chairs. Behind him is a doorway veiled by a heavy red curtain. Seeing him turn at the sound of our entrance, I realize now that he is blind.

Maite and I take the chairs in front of him, sitting down. His wife stands behind him, a hand on his shoulders, letting him know she is near.

"Sir, I want to thank you for inviting us to your beautiful home."

The lines on his face arc into a smile. "Yes, Pastor Roger, we are so glad you have come. I know you are wondering why I called you here to my house when I could have spoken to you at the prayer meeting. But I want to tell you a story."

He had called the day before to remind us to come, but we wouldn't have missed this meeting for anything. Maite and I edge forward on our chairs to hear him.

"Thirty years ago, I made a lot of money in Macau. God has blessed me. But the Holy Spirit told me to withhold some of the money, because He would have me release it later. I believe this is the time."

After he pats his wife's hand, she disappears behind the red curtain and comes back holding a cloth bag. She proceeds to pour out the contents onto a cloth on a table. A profusion of gold coins comes pouring out. Maite and I are speechless.

"Jesus wants you to have that building." Scooping the coins back into the bag, she places it in my hands. Maite's look of amazement mirrors my own.

"Do not wait for a good exchange rate," her husband instructs us.

I am still dumbstruck.

The wife places a hand on the bag of gold coins I am holding as if in a blessing. "You go and buy that building for Jesus."

After hurrying down the steps, we are in shock as we get in the car.

"Who has bags of gold?" Maite asks, laughing. The bag in her lap, she presses her hands against the sides of her head and says, through her giggles, "This is crazy. What is going on?"

We hug each other and then nervously make our way to the financial district. Who is this crazy God we are serving? Who sets aside bags of gold for thirty years?

As if God has not outdone Himself already, the miracles seem to snowball, gaining momentum, propelling us forward.

There is a dip in the real-estate market and the Musicians Union is losing money hand over fist. They lower the price of 230 Jones to $660,000.

At the same time, the district sells a property and one of the executive officers calls to let us know that they are tithing the sale of the property to our center in the amount of $100,000.

A few weeks later, this same officer takes a new position with our denomination loan program. He calls me again, asking, "Roger, do you feel God has called you to the Tenderloin?"

"Yes." My heart is pounding.

"How long will you be staying there?"

"As long as I can … forever."

There is a pause on the line. "We will give you the loan."

Forty days of fasting. Countless prayers. Mind-blowing miracles. And 230 Jones is ours.

■ ■ ■

A thousand people, mostly residents of the Tenderloin, line the streets in front of 230 Jones Street. The building stands behind us as a trophy of God's huge provision and grace. Maite and the kids are near me. A spirit of celebration is in the air. There are shouts and whistles up and down the street.

"Everyone, I want to thank you for coming here today! Many of you know that our being here is a miracle. And you also know that we love the Tenderloin. This building is an answer to our prayers. Let's pray and thank God for giving us this place."

With the *amen*, more cheering and whistling breaks out.

We open the door to let the community see our new home. Only the years will tell the miracles that will take place in these walls. All the meals that will be served. The hearts that will be turned toward the light. The bodies that will be clothed. The love that will pour out from this building out into the streets.

Cleaning up after the celebration, I am exhausted. With joy. It is a good feeling. And my stomach is full. That is also a good feeling. Food has never tasted as good as it did when we ended the fast.

As I turn to lock the door to 230 Jones, I know one thing. It is only just the beginning. The beginning of a dream to plant roots in this community and bless them with God's love on a daily basis.

Our after-school program is growing.

The thrift store is busy every day with residents coming to see their needs met.

Our Homeless Café will be moved from 302 Eddy to 230 Jones, feeding ninety people at each meal.

The youth group is growing.

But there is always more to be done. And the first thing we are going to do in this miracle building of ours is start a school.

Chapter 15

PRAYING AND FASTING FOR A SCHOOL

San Francisco, 1999

Don't stop thinking about tomorrow.

Walking down the street toward 230 Jones from the parking garage, I see the children lining up on the sidewalks. They huddle together in the sputtering mist, hunched beneath their backpacks. Hopefully their rides will be here soon, before it really begins to rain. The streets are not as busy as usual, but I see a drug dealer making a sale to a black SUV near the bus stop. I shake my head. The things these kids see every day, the things they witness in the halls of their apartment buildings, the things they experience in their own homes are things children should never know about or see in their neighborhoods. You can see their soft eyes grow hard with the realities of life the older they get.

I lift a hand and wave to a Hispanic boy who has been coming to our after-school program lately.

"Hi, Pastor Roger." He smiles, shyly. Color sweeps up his cheeks at being noticed.

"Are you coming to the after-school program today?"

"Yes!"

"Okay, we can look over that math, and we'll have a good snack, too!"

His brown eyes flicker up to meet mine, and he nods. I put my hand on his head and pray a silent blessing over him.

His brothers used to come to our Super Saturdays. They played dodge ball and heard stories about Jesus. But like so many kids around here, they are casualties of their environment.

Families fall apart in the Tenderloin. Mothers get caught up in prostitution. Absentee fathers get lost in drugs and crime. Left unattended, the pull of the gangs can be too strong for these kids. On the streets, where fear rules and parents are few and far between, the gangs are protection, a family of sorts. Kids often drop out of school after eighth grade and slip into a lifestyle of petty crime and easy drugs that only ends in pain and heartache. I shoot silent prayers to God on behalf of these children.

I have been praying for these kids for years. The odds are stacked against them. Survival is their main goal. Children go hungry every day in these apartment buildings. A lot of the kids in the Tenderloin are raising themselves. Getting themselves up and dressed each morning. Feeding themselves breakfast if they can find food in the apartment. They even have to get themselves out to the bus stop to be taken to school.

The fleet of yellow buses is coming up the street, breaking through the spitting mist. There are no public elementary schools in the Tenderloin. The children are bused to forty-two different schools around the city.

When I was an auditor, I used to get off work at about six or seven in the morning and drive through the Tenderloin. Children would be lined up in different spots waiting for school buses to come and transport them. I would stop and watch them from my car, thinking how that would not be allowed in the good neighborhoods around the city. Those parents would not let their children wait to go to school on the same street corner where drug lords and gangsters were. It's too dangerous and yet this is nothing new. The kids in the Tenderloin have always had it rough.

The fog and the cold and the filth make me want something more for these children. I pray for the kids I know by name as I continue up the street, "God, let these kids come to City Academy next year."

Pushing open the door to 230 Jones, I hear our students saying the Pledge of Allegiance. The school day has begun.

■ ■ ■

It is the needs of this community that drive me to my knees every day. How can you walk past an elderly person who is struggling to get their walker up on the curb and not stop to help them? Or pass by a man whose face is thin from lack of food and not hand him a sandwich? This is the feeling I get when I walk these blocks and look into the faces that pass me by. All around me, day in and day out, I see faces that are hurting. Faces that are pinched with hunger and faces that are drawn with fear. I see weary faces that have slept out on the street all night and faces that are vacant and forlorn, caught in the trap of mental illness. Then there are the faces that are hard with anger and the greedy faces of the pleasure seekers looking for the next high or the newest sex club. There is so much despair and depravity. And any one of these needy people could be my son, my daughter, my cousin, my auntie, my uncle.

How do we break this cycle of poverty and impoverished souls? It seems to me that it begins with the children. It is those who have been crushed by life, year after year, who continue on in the path of pain that poverty offers. What if we could meet these children, who have so much stacked against them at the beginning of their lives, and take them in, feed them, give them clothes, and surround them with the rich love of Jesus on a daily basis? This is the prayer that I prayed for seven years. *God, help me start a school for these kids. I don't know how to do it but You do.*

■ ■ ■

I ask my daughter Marie France to start the school for me. Marie France and her husband, Clint, have come up to the Tenderloin from Bethany where Clint is finishing up some classes before returning overseas to play professional basketball. She is sitting in the Good News Tenderloin Center folding fliers that ask for support for an upcoming event.

"Marie France, I have a job for you to do."

"Sure. What do you need?" She sets aside the stack of papers she is working on and looks up at me.

"I want you to start a school."

Her eyebrows lift.

"I want you to start a school here for the kids in the Tenderloin."

"I don't know how to start a school." The look she is giving me is reminiscent of her mother. "I'm just a teacher. That's not something I know how to do."

"Marie France, you know these kids. They need a place to be safe."

She looks down to fold another flier. "Where would we even have it?"

"We can start at 302, and as soon as we get 230 Jones, we will move it there."

"Who is going to teach? How will you pay someone to do that?"

"I will worry about that. You just figure out what we need to do to get it going, and we'll take care of the rest. These kids need a place to learn. Super Saturdays are not enough. We'll start small. You can do it. I know you can."

Marie France is shaking her head, her curls falling in her face. "We are going overseas as soon as Clint's contract comes in."

"You start it and then I can keep it going."

She lifts her head to look me in the eye. I know her heart. It is too soft toward these kids she loves. She can't say no. A smile is on her lips. She shakes her head one more time. "Okay. Let's do it."

I grin from ear to ear.

■ ■ ■

I hear laughter as I enter the room. Maite and Marie France are excited. I can tell by the way their smiles mirror each other's.

"Roger, you have to hear this." Maite beckons me over. "Marie France was just telling me about the group of pastors she just met with."

Marie France is still laughing. She has been working, networking, and planning the opening of the school for the past year. She had been asked to meet with a group of pastors from our area to tell them about the school. Fund-raising isn't something anyone in our family enjoys. It has been stressful, and it is good to see her smile.

"You know I didn't want to go talk to all those pastors and ask them for money for the school, right?"

"Right."

"But the night before I had to meet with them I had a dream."

"A dream?"

"Yes. I dreamed that I found myself at the scene of this big building that was a theater, and there were two lines of children entering the theater. One line was full of normal, happy, healthy kids. They would walk up to the ticket booth of this theater and hand in their ticket and walk into the theater. Then there was this other group, this other line of kids entering this same theater. I looked across, and I recognized them to be the kids at the Tenderloin, for whatever reason. A little bit lost, no parents around. Just different colored faces, and I knew those were the Tenderloin kids. When they would walk up to the ticket counter, they had no ticket, and there would be a pause. They would stand there, and two dark figures would come upon them and start beating them up and dragging them into the theater."

Concern lines her forehead as she is telling me the dream.

"One after the other, the Tenderloin kids would walk up. They didn't have a ticket, and they would get harassed and attacked and dragged into the theater. It was like the payment for them to get in was their suffering. I was frantic. I kept trying to grab kids and put them in the other line, but then I would walk up to the ticket counter, and I didn't have enough money. I would have only enough money for a couple of kids. It was horrible."

"It sounds horrible." I can picture it all too easily. Marie France is describing the hopelessness these kids feel each day just trying to survive in this area.

"I felt like I had to tell people about the kids in this other line that need us to take them and give them a safe education, spiritual love, everything they need. So I shared the dream with the pastors."

"What happened?"

Marie France's smile grows wider. "They are going to help us. I already received some pledges to support some of the kids."

It is beginning. The prayers for the last seven years are starting to be answered. When I pray and fast, I don't always know when the answer will come. I just know it will come.

But even more amazing with this prayer is that the dream that has been growing in my heart, culminating for all these years, is culminating in my daughter's heart as well. Seeing her joy, her hope, her courage moves me. I am seeing her step out and grow, stretching herself on behalf of this dream.

When Marie France and Clint leave for his basketball season, I pick up where she has left off.

■ ■ ■

Life changes quickly in the Tenderloin. It seems like we turned around twice and our children have become adults. Michelle is in her second year of college at Bethany College. Her joy for life and her love of life is evident. Phil married a beautiful girl, Rossie, one of our Tenderloin volunteers, and moved to her home state of Montana to start their family. Marie France and Clint have already been married for four years and are following their dreams of teaching and playing basketball. At eighteen, Chris is leading our youth group and is our worship leader. Seeing him, so young, leading, lighting up the room with his laughter, he fills us with joy. All of our kids do.

They have all spent countless hours on these streets, seeing the needs and hurts of this community. They have played in the run-down ballroom of the Cadillac Hotel and passed out food to hungry families. They have set up chairs and passed out fliers and been cranky when we stayed too late and did too many outreaches. They have watched us agonize over ministry decisions and make mistakes. Each one of them has spent countless family weekends in the service of others.

We know that our passion for the poor has shaped them, but we don't know if the path God has for them winds through the Tenderloin. In our heart of hearts, it is our dream that our children will join us in the ministry, pouring out their lives in the Tenderloin with us. But we also know that they need to spread their wings and follow their own dreams and passions. We keep our prayers to ourselves but moments like that moment with Marie France lift us and spur us on to dream more about what it would be like to have them working with us.

We open our school with one teacher, a gifted young man named Calvin, and an aide. And seven kindergarten students. The following June is one of our proudest moments.

Marie France and Clint are back for the summer. The main room of 302 Eddy has been arranged for our very first kindergarten graduation. There are bright balloons and a hand-painted banner covers the wall, saying, "We've had a great year!"

Four parents and a handful of volunteers from our center form the audience. Marie France, seven months pregnant, stands near the podium as each of the kindergarteners parades in front of the audience. She is smiling almost as big as her mother and I are.

"We are so proud of these kids. They did great their first year here at the San Francisco City Academy. We are thankful that God has brought each one of them here. Let's give them a hand."

Scroll in hand, she calls the first student forward. A sweet boy with dark wavy hair and a big grin holds out a chubby hand for his kindergarten diploma. As Marie France bends down to hug him, her belly gets in the way. He races back to his chair, causing laughter to ripple through the small crowd. The dream has come true.

None of us has any idea of what is about to happen in the next few years. Sometimes dreams can take a while to come in to their fullness.

Running the school is not my greatest gifting. I am not an educator. But the dream has not changed. The children in the Tenderloin are still suffering, needing what is not being given to them in other schools. We still long to nurture them, body, mind, and spirit, giving them a good start in this hard life.

When Marie France and Clint rejoin us after years overseas, we have the perfect administrator. She is a smart and godly young lady, and she truly cares for each and every child. We hire new teachers, who work for a fraction of what they could get elsewhere, who pour their hearts and lives out for the kids. God is good. Miracle is laid upon miracle. Hope upon hope. Prayer upon prayer.

We begin to build a safe place in the heart of the city for its most precious residents. The children. Little do we know that in a few short years all of our dreams for a school in the Tenderloin will be at risk.

The path that God has set me on is not always clear. But I know that if I chase Him, if I spend time praying and laying down my desires before Him, He never fails me. Throughout the years He has shown Himself to me over and over again. Our practice of fasting and prayer is about to open doors for us that I would have never imagined, never dreamed of.

It all begins with a prayer for a tiny run-down park in the middle of San Francisco.

Chapter 16

PRAYING AND FASTING
FOR THE TENDERLOIN

Tenderloin, 2004
A thirty-three-day hunger strike for the Tenderloin

Syringes in the sand. Drug deals going down near the community center. Addicts sitting on the ledge surrounding the park. Gangsters hanging out, playing basketball.

Hands on the black bars surrounding Boeddeker Park, I study the park playground at the corner of Jones and Eddy. I turn and look over my shoulder across the street toward the City Academy. Soon the students will come across the street to play here. The sun has burned through the morning fog and is warming the air. This park is the only park, the only patch of green in the Tenderloin. A small playground with a worn-out play structure is tucked into the corner of the park, bordered by a pathway leading up its center. A grouping of trees and a drooping garden fill in the back corner across from the community center. Multiple basketball courts line the front of the space. A high wrought-iron fence encloses the whole park, marking out its small territory in the midst of the chaos and business of the Tenderloin.

This park has great possibilities. It has been the staging ground for several of our events over the years. Clint has packed the basketball courts with children for sports camps, filling the air with their laughter and excitement as he teaches them the fundamentals of basketball along with telling stories about Jesus.

We have gathered large groups of volunteers here on Thanksgiving and Christmas to pass out hundreds of yellow grocery bags full of fresh produce and canned goods. We rented out the community center to assemble thousands of hot meals. After instructions and prayer, hundreds of men, women, and children carrying hot meals and grocery bags left the park to go into the surrounding buildings. They distributed much-needed nutrition, encouragement, and hope to those who often have too little food to eat and more despair than we can imagine.

I sigh, leaning into the bars, feeling the cool metal against my forehead. Beer bottles butt up against the fence along with soiled napkins and soda cans. *I wonder when Parks and Rec last cleaned up in here.* A young man with a scraggly beard mutters to himself as he sits near me on the ledge that surrounds the park. He grows agitated when I look over at him. I can't tell if he is on something or if he struggles with mental illness.

Pushing away from the bars, I head back toward 230 Jones. *We'll have to make sure to check for drug paraphernalia before the kids play today.*

That isn't the only thing worrying me today. The real problem on this street is the new club going in. To our delight, the bar next to the school had shut down a few months earlier. To our dismay, it is reopening as a strip club.

I pause in front of the storefront. A construction worker with a bucketful of debris steps out of the door in front of me. It is bad enough that the kids have to deal with the residue from all the gangs and drug addicts in the area. It is another thing for them to be exposed to a sex club each time they walk to school. There is a slow-burning anger roiling inside me. This is more than just another court date for my calendar.

For the past few years, I have been going to court and opposing each new liquor license coming up for review in the Tenderloin. The normal number of liquor licenses in San Francisco is twenty-five per square mile. The last one we fought was the forty-ninth to be located in the Tenderloin.

A light breeze sends a Styrofoam cup scuttling down the sidewalk next to me. The amount of trash littering the streets seems to be growing with the years. Pushing through the door of 230 Jones, I pass the elevator and take the stairs. The dimly lit stairwell only dampens my spirits. No one cares about these streets. No one protects these kids from seeing what they shouldn't. No one cares about this corner of San Francisco with its seedy shops and run-down buildings. It shows just by walking down the street. Somebody has to do something.

Maite seems to think that somebody is me.

"Roger, you know you have to do something." Her eyes flash with the anger I have been feeling inside all day.

We face each other in the office. Her arms crossed, she takes a deep breath and waits for my answer. It is unbelievable, really. Anywhere else in America, having a sex club next to an elementary school would be unthinkable. But this is the Tenderloin, the underbelly of San Francisco. *Who cares really?*

I feel the familiar tug in my spirit. *This one only comes by prayer and fasting.*

I groan inside. Fasting is never easy. But it is necessary.

"I know," I answer. I lower myself into the chair. The morning sun slants through the window across my desk. A thought is forming, shaping itself in my mind. "I'm tired of this. Of having to fight for every single thing. These kids shouldn't have to put up with this. They should have a safe neighborhood. A good place to live, like everyone else."

Maite nods, sitting down next to me. "What are you going to do?"

"The strip club isn't the only thing that needs to change around here. If we are going to ask the city to step in and do something, we are going to ask for all the changes that need to be made."

Maite sits down at the computer. A cup of coffee at her elbow, she begins to type as I speak.

"We need the streets cleaned. And not just once a week. Every day. We need that French Porta Potty gone or at least patrolled by the police. No one uses it as a restroom. The drug addicts just use it to get high. We need more police in the neighborhood."

The requests come to mind so easily. They are so obvious, so needed in this community.

"We need something done about the ledge around the park. There are always homeless guys or drug addicts surrounding the park on the ledge. We need them off of there. These kids need to feel safe in this park. They need to feel like they can go there without being scared or bothered. There needs to be a community association that has a say as to what kinds of businesses are allowed in this neighborhood. And we need a law saying that no sex clubs can be located next to a school or church."

I rub my hands together and then fold them. It's time to put feet to our many prayers that have assaulted the heavens over the years. This isn't the first time we have taken action when we have prayed over our city.

This year I decided to do what the leaders in the Old Testament did. I took a day and walked the entire circumference of San Francisco's twenty-eight miles, circling the city in prayer. It was a marathon walk of prayer to ask God to show mercy on this city. I took a day to walk the Tenderloin. To stand in front of each illicit establishment—whether it was a massage parlor, a liquor store, or an underground marijuana club—and asked God to close it down. There are 110 such establishments in this square mile. The next day I walked another sixteen miles, praying over each neighborhood in San Francisco, twenty-seven in all, begging for God's stirring and revival to break out in that area. I prayed over the entrance to the city, that God would keep evil from its gates and clean up the city. Like Joshua, I have marched the length of this great city—this city that I love and long for—and prayed for God's power to overcome. I have prayed for God to shake loose the foundations of indifference and chaos that surround this city like a wall, and that His mercy and grace would pour in and draw people to Him. God is not finished with this golden city. He is only beginning to move. Maite and I know it is coming.

There needs to be a change in our neighborhood. A huge change. But both of us know that none of this is going to happen unless God is behind it. Fighting some of the politicians at City Hall with their slick smiles and carefully crafted answers is not going to be easy, but we have had twenty years of seeing God do things that people said He could not do. We know He is bigger and more powerful than we can imagine. We just have to pray and wait on Him. He will do the work.

Maite finishes the letter that contains the changes we want made in the Tenderloin and we address it to the city supervisors and the mayor. To make sure they are received and read, our friend, a former chaplain, hand-delivers them.

The chaplain, a retired Bank of America employee, represents us well. An African-American gentleman filled with poise and dignity, the chaplain decided to join his prayers to ours and live out his faith in the halls of 230 Jones Street. He lived on the third floor for several years, ministering with us and loving the people of the Tenderloin. The day before my planned hunger strike, he mounted the steps of the capital and visited the mayor's office and each supervisor's office, leaving the letter that states the changes we seek and informs them of the hunger strike that will be taking place in the piazza across from City Hall. He let them know I would be there until the changes were made.

The next day breaks cold and clear with a breeze that lifts the morning fog blowing off of the bay. The capitol looms large across the piazza. San Francisco City Hall reminds me of a scaled-down version of our nation's capitol. Its gleaming white structure is held up by impressive pillars and topped by a gleaming, golden dome.

I am sitting in the piazza across from City Hall. I had an omelet for breakfast. It will be my last meal until we begin to see some changes in the Tenderloin. I am dwarfed by the majestic building behind me and take a seat on the plastic folding chair that I have brought with me. I take a sip from a chilled water bottle and set it down next to me on the concrete. A white poster board sign is taped to the back of my chair and a matching sign hangs around my neck. Both say Hunger Strike. I am in this for the long haul.

It seems that God likes to use the foolish things, the weak things of the world, to shame the wise and powerful. Something unseen is set in motion when I stop eating. At first no one notices me. I am just another bum sitting across from City Hall.

This slab of concrete has become my temporary home. The public square is my bedroom. My black jacket is my blanket as I pass each night laid out on the ground with my face pressed against the concrete. I don't eat. I don't shower. I just sit and watch and pray and wait for God to make His move.

Maite comes and sits with me during the day. Two weeks in finds us sitting together on a dreary morning. The sky mirrors my emotional state. I feel depressed. This happens when I fast for long lengths of time. I know it shows on my face.

"How are you doing, Roger? Are you okay?" Maite's eyes show their concern. She hands me a new bottle of water.

"I'm okay." I take the bottle and hold her hand. Her nearness is always a comfort. The warmth of her hand clasped in mine lifts my spirits.

I hear someone approaching, and I look up to see the mayor. Maybe he has read the letter. He looks suave with his hair slicked back and his custom suit. A definite contrast to the black pants and black Windbreaker I have on. He reaches out his hand to shake mine. A few men gather with him. This is the first time he has talked to me.

"Hey, I read your letter, Pastor Huang. I understand your concerns for your community. I just want you to know that I would like to make these changes you are asking for. But one thing we just can't do is shut down the strip club. Apparently it is the first of its kind in San Francisco. It is a historical landmark." His tone is warm and understanding, but I know he can see my displeasure as I squint up at him. "Tell you what, why don't you let me buy you some pizza and we can work on these other requests."

I shift in my chair. The morning is cold and wisps of fog still straggle across the sky. The wind whips at my face and blows at Maite's hair. It penetrates my coat, chilling me to the marrow of my bones. I am tired and emotionally worn-out. And the hunger pangs at the mention of pizza are significant.

"Listen, Mr. Mayor, I would love to have pizza, but I really can't eat until all these things happen. I know you can understand that. These things are really important to our community. For the kids. For our school."

He takes a step back and mutters something to one of his aides. Who knows what they are thinking at this point?

"Okay, Pastor Huang. We will see what we can do. I really wish you would eat something."

I know that no politician wants a man starving on his doorstep. It's not good for their image.

"Thank you for coming to talk to me." I smile again. I don't know what God is doing, but I know He is doing something.

I watch them head back up the steps, their heads bent in conversation. The weeks pass. Word spreads of the hunger strike. People start showing up to gawk. News reporters are following the story. The health department begins sending someone to regularly check my blood pressure and bring me Gatorade. My blood pressure is beginning to drop a little. My body shows signs of weakening.

The breakthrough comes on the thirty-third day. I notice a cluster of reporters gathering on the steps of City Hall ten feet from me. My thirty-third day without a morsel to eat. My thirty-third day without a shower. But God has moved again. Ask anyone involved in politics. Getting policy changed in a month is unheard of. But that is what is happening.

The mayor descends the steps and starts to speak to the reporters. "We are calling it Operation Scrub Down." He proceeds to list off every item on my list: street cleaners, a neighborhood alliance, and increased police patrols.

Maite leans toward me as we listen to him address the press. "Roger, the streets have already been washed this morning, and Public Works is already putting in rebar around the ledge."

Word has come that the owner of the building that houses the strip club wants to sell to us.

A neighborhood care group has been formed, giving the community a say in what kinds of new businesses can fill its storefronts.

One of the city supervisors has passed new legislation: no adult entertainment can be within one thousand feet of a school or church.

In the 150 years of the city's existence, no law like this has ever passed in San Francisco.

"Roger, it's time to come home. God has done it! Everything we asked has been done." Maite's smile is beautiful in the dazzling light of the sun.

I pick up my chair and bottle of water. Once again, God has done the impossible. In His provision and mercy, He has turned the hearts of the powerful toward us to use their influence to help the Tenderloin.

Looking back on those days, it is hard to believe what took place. God always overwhelms us when He moves in His power. We haven't slacked off in love or care of the streets. We are still vigilant in our prayers for the Tenderloin. We changed the name of our growing ministry to City Impact. We want to impact this city with the greatness of God's love.

We walk the streets praying for His power and peace to be released in every borough, precinct, and neighborhood. This year will mark our eighth year of walking twenty-eight miles around the city, praying for our neighborhood and praying for illicit businesses to close. Fifteen businesses have closed so far. More than one of the owners has come to know Christ.

Although the owner of the building that housed the strip club retracted his offer to sell, he died suddenly within six months of the thirty-three-day hunger strike. The strip club and his cocktail lounge closed down. A Thai restaurant has replaced the lounge.

As we anoint the curbs of our neighborhoods with oil and pray for the people of this city, our heart cry is the same: *God, show these people Your love and Your mercy.* We have experienced it for ourselves so many times in numerous ways. We can't help but believe He wants to do the same for those who live in the Tenderloin.

We are always amazed and thankful when God works in our lives. He continues to blow us away with His provision and creativity. Time after time, He surprises us and overwhelms us with His generosity. Even when our prayers turn from the ministry in the Tenderloin toward our personal desires or needs.

One of the things I have always longed for is a place of my own … a place of permanence. I never thought, being an inner-city worker in one of the poorest neighborhoods in our city, that I would own a home. But I prayed for one anyway. Because I know that the God I love and chase after knows my heart and the dreams and hopes I have. But God doesn't always answer our prayers the way we ask Him to. God didn't give me a home. He gave me three.

Chapter 17

PRAYING AND FASTING
FOR HOMES

Sunset District, 2005
I need a home to get the job done.

A breeze has blown the fog off of Ocean Beach along the Great
Highway. The gulls are diving after fish as I jog down the path along
the beach. Strands of seaweed litter the sand, and a yellow dog darts
back and forth toward the sweeping surf, barking as if he can catch it.

Early morning is my favorite time to run.

I am running, thinking about the day ahead, praying, mull-
ing over the next step. I breathe in and out rhythmically as my feet
pound the gravel path. A cool sweat covers me. Somehow the mix of
the salt air and cold wind clears my mind. I can't believe I am here,
jogging on this path only blocks from our new home. Sometimes
God overwhelms us with His goodness. Moving from Daly City to a
house near the beach was an answer to years of prayer and fasting. In

the right moment in the right time, God's provision amazed us. He went over the top this time.

Our first home in Daly City was a miracle in its own right. Looking at our finances, we should have never even been able to own a home. But when our landlord in San Francisco called us on Father's Day and told us that he needed us to move out of the house, the search was on.

We were renting in the Sunset District, but we started looking and praying for any house God might have for us. Maite called me one day with a lead.

"Roger, I found a house on Callan Street in Daly City with a lease-to-buy option. I think we should go check it out." We fasted during the days leading up to our viewing appointment.

Driving from San Francisco to Daly City, we hit a dreary bank of fog. The small blue house was located on the corner of a three-way stop directly behind a bus stop. The exterior was weathered and a little run-down. That didn't quite prepare us for what we would find inside. This house had seen some hard living.

Maite and I walked through the kitchen, the living room, and the bedrooms taking it all in. Outdated lighting cast shadows on the dark walls. The carpet was dingy and worn. The bathrooms had seen better days. This home gave new meaning to the word *fixer-upper*. The entire house shuddered as a low-flying jet passed overhead. At the sound, Maite looked at the eighty-year-old owner, but he seemed unconcerned.

We found out later that the house is directly under the path of San Francisco International Airport air traffic.

I looked out the window to the murky fog outside. A block away, I could see the hazy outline of the entrance to the Chinese cemetery.

I was not sure that a house could get more depressing than that. *Is this dismal little home what God has for us?*

Maite opened a dank cupboard in the cramped kitchen. Her nose wrinkled up. Sometimes God answers our prayers in a way that requires us to get our hands dirty. We have never been put off by hard work before. We decided to take the lease.

■ ■ ■

A year is up before we know it, and we have the opportunity to buy the house. Maite and I are torn. We have to make a decision whether we want to buy the house or not. It's doubtful if renovations will ever be complete. The house is still depressing at best. Even the birdhouse in the backyard has yet to attract a family of birds. A gray fog hangs over the backyard.

Maite looks out the window toward the birdhouse nestled in the trees. "Roger, the birds don't even want to live here. Even they are depressed by this house. The entire time we have lived here, we have never seen a bird even land on the perch. Maybe we should be like the birds and find another place to live."

I nod, thinking of all the ways this house doesn't meet our needs. The house is not in San Francisco. The work to fix it seems endless. The fog is depressing. I have to drive twenty minutes to the Great Highway to run by the beach and pray. More than that, we don't have good credit due to the constant financial struggle of surviving off of what we earn at the rescue mission. We have no money for a down payment.

Leaving here seems like a no-brainer.

Putting my hands behind my head, I sigh, feeling it down to the soles of my feet.

"Roger, I think we need a sign from God if we are supposed to buy this house. Let's ask God to send a bird to this birdhouse today if He wants us to buy this house."

I nod in agreement with her, brushing her hair back with my hand. "That would be a miracle, wouldn't it?"

Her smile is wide at the thought.

That evening, when we pull into the driveway and get out of the car, a soupy fog has begun hemming in the ends of the street. Another cold night in Daly City. We enter the house and Maite stops midroom. "You have got to be kidding."

I follow her gaze out the back window. The birdhouse is covered with birds. Not just one bird. Multiple birds. It is as if God wants to make sure we get the message. One bird is not enough. He has sent us a small flock. We both start laughing. This is the house He has for us.

We are amazed the following weeks as a friend of ours gives us ten thousand dollars for the down payment and as an impossible loan that leaves our loan officer shaking his head in disbelief is approved. Looking up from the stack of papers we just signed, he says, "God is with you, Mr. Huang. That's for sure."

We can't believe it. This is the first house we have ever owned. We've signed on the dotted line, and now we have to get back to renovating the house.

Renovations seem to be our path in life. Whether it is a run-down building or a run-down house or a run-down life, God has called Maite and me to a ministry of restoration. We find ourselves tearing out old infrastructures and infusing old buildings and weary people with new life. It might be a can of paint for a room. New cupboards for a kitchen. New light fixtures for the Homeless Café. Or a new outlook for a person seeking healing and wholeness in the Tenderloin.

More often than not, I find that the one who needs the most revamping is me. My soul. My outlook. My life. Countless times over the years, I have found myself broken and in need of God's restorative grace. Whether it is in my inability to communicate my feelings to Maite, my relationship challenges with my children, or unforgiveness toward my parents, I find myself on my knees or fasting, asking God for the change, the insight, or the healing I need.

Over the years, I have told my family of origin about God's love. One by one, I led my parents and brothers to the Lord. My sister also came to know the Lord through a friend. But the residue and pain of the years of abuse are hard to erase. I see the fruit of those abusive years played out in different ways in each of our lives.

We have never had that intimate connection that families can have. Prayer and fasting are the only things that seem to make those inroads into my soul, the only things that can reshape my wounded heart and bring new healing.

Maite is my constant companion, speaking truth to me, encouraging me, and fasting with me in each situation.

The other day a volunteer came up to me and was telling me how great I was and how I inspire her. I called Maite and told her, "There are some people here who think I am pretty amazing. I have fans."

It was quiet on the other end of the phone. Then she said, "Let them live with you for one day."

I had to laugh. She knows me. The ins and outs of my soul. My struggles with relationships and relating to people. She knows that even now I have to ask God daily to help me. And God always comes through for me, answering my prayers. More often than not showing me that through Him, with Him, all things are possible.

God tends to plant dreams in my heart that seem impossible. I take those dreams and turn them into prayers, placing them back in the hands of the One who can make them happen. Like the dream to have a prayer home of my own.

From the earliest days of my faith, getting away from the crush of everyday life and heading out to the woods or going to the ocean to pray has been a physical way to express to God that I am chasing after Him. Giving Him time and space to work in my life. More than anything, I wanted a place that was ours where I could go on a whim. A place of prayer and retreat that we could go to throughout the year to pray and fast. It was a thought, a hope that lingered in the back of my mind each time I went to the coast to pray. I tried to go once a month. It became a life-changing experience for me, taking time out to be with God one-on-one.

I am driving home one weekend after praying and fasting up near Fort Bragg when I see a For Sale sign on a large bluff overlooking the ocean. Pulling over, I get out of the car. Hiking through the waist-high grasses, the salt breeze blows through my hair and tugs at my Windbreaker. The bright sun warms my back and the wild flowers that litter the hillside. The scent of the sea mixes with the cool fragrance of the majestic Monterey cypress trees and tall pines that hedge in the property.

Reaching the top of the slope, I turn and look out at the Pacific. Immense. Grand. Vast. Its blue and green swells fold into frothy waves that crash on the small rocky beaches below and smash into the jutting cliffs, sending spray up the sides. My heart pounds in my chest, matching the thrum of the waves on the shore.

"God, if You give me this piece of land, I will build a prayer home here for You. I will come and pray and spend time with You. You know I will!"

Cars below me wind up the ribbon of Highway 1, which mirrors the curves of the coastline. Getting back in my car to head to San Francisco, I mull over the prayer in my mind. I don't know how God will possibly bring it about, but I trust Him with this desire, knowing that if it is from Him, it will come to pass.

■ ■ ■

Life at 230 Jones is always busy. Always. Thoughts crowd my mind. We are getting ready to buy the Callan Street house in Daly City. The school year is in full swing. More and more volunteers are showing up on our doorstep who need to be organized and utilized.

Shoving tables and chairs into place for a volunteer sign-in table, I pause to take a breath.

We are getting ready for another street event. The streets are cordoned off, and volunteers surround me. The shouts of the schoolkids getting out of school are ringing in the hallways.

Farther down the hallway, I can hear the faint ringing of the phone.

"You guys finish up and I will be right back," I call over my shoulder as I head down the hall and grab the phone.

"Roger?"

"Yes, this is Roger."

"This is Jack from Fort Bragg."

"Jack, how are you?" I ask enthusiastically. I met Jack and his wife in Fort Bragg years before through a mutual friend during one of my prayer and fasting times in Albion. They let us use their huge home in Fort Bragg to host kids camps in the summer. We would load thirty to forty kids and eight leaders into cars and vans and leave the cramped streets of the Tenderloin for the woodsy beach town of Fort Bragg. The redwoods and pine forests are only miles from the beach. Up a one-lane road nestled on a hillside is a huge house tucked under a canopy of pines. We invade the house, filling it with laughter and excited children. The kids run down into the pasture, play games, eat s'mores around the campfire, and take trips down to the beach. It is a kid's dream come true. Seeing the children free of their worry, breathing in the sea air, and running free with abandon brings me a joy I can't describe. Because of Jack's generosity this is possible.

"What can I do for you?"

"Roger, I want you to have the house."

I am stunned. Silent. "What?"

"I would like for you to have the house. I want to sell it to you."

"Jack, I'm overwhelmed by your generosity, but you know we don't have money to buy the house from you."

Jack laughs. "It's okay. I know how you get money. You'll figure it out. I am leaving the keys for you."

We talk a few minutes more. I am still stunned. I hang up the phone and walk back down the hallway.

The center is buzzing with activity. Maite is in one corner setting up a hospitality table for the volunteers, arranging cookies and drinks to refresh them.

"Maite …"

She looks up at me, still fiddling with a plate of cookies.

"That was Jack on the phone. He wants us to have the house."

"What?"

"Yeah, he said we can have it. We're going to work out the cost. I think he means he wants us to pray and fast the money in."

Maite sits down on a folding chair next to the hospitality table. Volunteers crowd down the hall toward the door.

For a moment time stands still.

Her eyes mirror my own disbelief. A house on the coast for us. To pray in. To have camps in. To meet with God. God didn't just give me a piece of property. He gave me a house along with it. He astounds me with His generosity. We can't help grinning at each other.

"That's crazy!"

"I know."

We laugh like a pair of teenagers with a secret and head out after the volunteers to join the event.

■ ■ ■

We drive up that weekend, windows down. The peacefulness and hope of what is taking place permeates the car. Following the coastline, we drive past the Cliff House and cross the wide bridge that arches over Noyo Harbor and leads into the sleepy town of Fort Bragg. The sun has already gone down, and the moon is shining out over the water. The expanse of ocean is dark, and the dim lights of buoys and trawlers dot the inky waves.

Passing through the center of town, the road moves into the country, and we are winding our way toward the next small beach town. Turning up a hill and into the long drive, we arrive. Excited. Unbelieving. Hopeful.

The house is pitch-black and unlocked when we try the front door. We let ourselves in. No one is home. All six thousand square feet of the house awaits us. I let out a breath and flip on the lights. Walking cautiously over to the entrance, I see a square piece of paper sitting on the floor, the house keys next to it. Reaching to pick it up, I hold it up to the light. It reads, "Roger, take the home and make an offer when you can. —Jack."

Placing the note in Maite's hands, I watch as she reads it.

"Roger, this is amazing...."

"I know. I can't believe it."

The house is ours. We call it the Blessing Home. It blesses every person who walks through its doors. Like our other home, this one calls for renovations too, but I am so excited by the fact that God has answered this prayer in such a tangible way, I can hardly contain my joy.

It seems a pattern is set. Each time we need a home—for ourselves, for our staff—the door is opened. Homes for the teachers at our school. Homes for our kids. Homes for the staff who devote their lives and talents twenty-four hours a day, seven days a week, to the people of the Tenderloin. It doesn't usually happen in the way we think it will, but God is always creative and surprises us. Loans come through. Favor is found.

At the height of the dot-com boom, we sell the Callan Street home for a $400,000 profit and are able to buy a three-story home in the Sunset District. A home only blocks from the Great Highway and my favorite place to run. The home that gives respite from the hectic life and ministry in the Tenderloin.

Looking at all the homes we have been able to buy over the years, my son Chris once said, "Dad, you are the poorest rich man I have ever met."

And it's true. In His generosity, God has overwhelmed us time and again. And not just with homes. But with people. In the craziest of situations, God has sent people to us to join in our work, meet our needs, and completely astonish us with their love for the people of the Tenderloin. The people He uses never cease to amaze me.

I guess I should know that the God who brings the right house at the right time would always bring the right people at the right time. One of these people came from the East Bay on a whim and set a chain of events in motion that would shape our future as a ministry. It all started with a marathon and baggy full of money.

Chapter 18

PRAYING AND FASTING FOR A BUILDING PROJECT

230 Jones Street, 2007
A man from God with a ten-million-dollar project

"I'm sorry, Pastor Huang. But this is your last warning. If you can't get this building up to code, we are going to have to shut the school down."

The fire inspector fills the hallway with his presence. His dark uniform seems out of place against the wall plastered with the students' colorful artwork.

"It is not safe, and I would be doing you and the children a great disservice if I let you keep using the building in this condition."

He finishes writing out his observations on his clipboard and tears off the sheet, pressing it into my hand. A look of seriousness pulls his forehead into a frown. A feeling of dread washes over me. I know he does not want to shut us down. I also know that he takes the safety of the children seriously. This is not his first visit. We have been written up several times. There just isn't any way to fund these types of repairs.

"Okay. Thank you, Inspector. We will get it taken care of."

He shakes my hand and walks down the hall, through the maze of small offices, toward the front door of 230 Jones.

"We'll be back in touch soon," he says, turning to look over his shoulder at me.

That is what I'm afraid of.

Our miracle building is in bad shape. Built in 1924 as the Musicians Union building, it has seen better days. The basement was a speakeasy during the prohibition and now houses our after-school programs. The first through third floors are a hodgepodge of offices and larger rooms, each one showing the wear of constant use throughout the years. We use them for classrooms, offices, and housing for our staff. Every corner of the building needs refurbishing and tender care, from paint to plumbing.

But the pressing concerns are the fire-code violations we were written up for: a sprinkler system needed throughout the building; a retrofitted back staircase; an alarm system in case of fire. All in all, a couple of hundred thousands dollars' worth of renovations.

We are struggling just to get our energy bill paid each month. Hundreds of thousands of dollars are not something we have on hand. A sense of desperation is building in my chest. The weight of this visit settles on my shoulders.

One of the students passes me in the hallway. "Hi, Pastor Roger." Her small round face lights up at me.

"Hello!" I brush the top of her head with my palm as she passes by me. *What is going to happen to these kids if we have to close the school?*

Holding the paper in my hand, I walk around the building, noting each crack, each broken fixture, each dingy mark on the wall. Each floor has a mile-long checklist of repairs that should be made. The air is stale and I can hardly breathe. I shove the list of violations in my pocket.

How can we do this? How can we come up with this kind of money?

Maite and I have been fasting two or three days a week for the past year. The constant stress of our ministry keeps us on our knees. The struggle to keep the school and rescue mission financially afloat is a daily worry, a weekly battle. Each bill, each cost, weighs on us.

Not only do the buildings need to be kept up and supplies purchased, but the staff needs to be paid. Each family, each staff member is already stretched to the limit with the minimal pay they get. They are pouring their lives out here, and we know they sacrifice just as we do.

"God, I don't know what to do. Where do I get $200,000? I don't know anyone who can help me. We are in a sinkhole here. Can't You help us?"

Entering the kitchen, I go to the fridge, pulling out an armful of vegetables. Dinner for the Homeless Café won't fix itself. Chopping and dicing gets out some of my frustration.

Prayers work their way into dinner prep frequently in this kitchen. "God, what are we going to do?"

There is no answer, just the whir of the cars running the length of the street outside the window. There are still so many prayers to be answered. The police station across the street has cleaned up the gangs off the corners a little, but pools of homeless people still huddle in front of stores on wet winter days. Teenagers, strung out and hopeless, still find their way to Eddy and Jones every year. Human trafficking is still thriving in the massage parlors. Refugee families still crowd the high-rise apartment buildings and struggle to survive in this foreign country. These are the people I love. My heart aches for them. I know God has given us this building to use to minister to the poor in a hundred different ways. Why does it feel like it is all crumbling beneath us no matter how hard we try to keep it going?

Laying down the knife, I lean over the counter. Head in my hands, whispered prayers slip from my lips. Tears crowd the back of my eyelids. God knows my heart. That every child, every youth, every adult in the Tenderloin would come to know Him. He also knows that we can't do this ministry alone. We need people to come alongside us, lift our arms up, hold us up in prayer, and invest in the lives we are touching.

"God, there has to be someone who can help us!"

A name weaves its way into my prayers. *Laura.*

I stop midprayer. *Laura? The housewife from Danville?*

Earlier in the year, we had met several women from Community Presbyterian Church in Danville. Susan, a church member and the first to hear of our ministry, invited us to her home for a prayer meeting on her birthday. Through her, we met Marsha. When businessman Tom Down gave CPC $10,000 in one-hundred-dollar bills to give to its members as seed money to invest in different ministries, Marsha brought us her $100. She felt that God was telling her to, so she had driven all the way from East Bay to deliver the money. Through the same church, we met Laura, a vivacious blonde who was excited about God and what He was doing at City Impact.

A new believer, she was drawn in by our story, so she ran a marathon to raise money for us. During my visit to Community Presbyterian Church, she came to me with a baggy full of money in hand. Her blonde hair was swept into a ponytail, and she had a wistful smile on her face. "I tried to run the full marathon, but I couldn't make it. Here is the money I raised. I want to do everything I can to help."

I was touched by her sincerity. The baggy of both bills and coins was heavy in my palm. "Thanks so much, Laura. Every bit counts."

It was in these small moments, with these unique people, that a connection to this church was born. Our lives became interwoven with this church across the bay, but we didn't yet realize it. God was laying a framework of people and hope and relationship that He would build upon in the coming years.

I shake my head and keep pacing the floor. *Surely the answer to the huge problem we have with this broken-down building is not a stay-at-home mom in Danville. Or is it?*

Of all the people I have known throughout the years and who have supported this ministry, Laura is the one who keeps coming to mind.

Leaving the kitchen, I go to my office to make the call, shutting the door behind me. I can't believe what I'm about to do. My heart is racing and my hands shake a little as I pick up the phone. *Okay, God, if this is who You want me to call, I will call her.*

The phone rings three times. With each ring, my heart pounds harder in my chest.

"Hello?" Her voice is vibrant over the phone line.

"Hi, Laura, this is Pastor Roger from City Impact in San Francisco. Do you remember me? I met you when you brought us the money you raised from the marathon you ran."

"Pastor Roger, it's so good to hear from you! Of course, I remember you. How are you doing?"

Rubbing my forehead with my hand, I sit back down on the folding chair. The fog-darkened room feels dark in more ways than one.

"Listen, Laura, I have something I need to tell you. I have been praying about our building. We need help with it, and your name is the one that comes to mind."

There is a pause on the other end. "How can I help you, Pastor Roger?"

"I don't know how to say this…. Our building is in a lot of trouble. We have several violations with the fire inspector, and if we don't get them fixed, they are going to shut the school down. I was wondering if you would be willing to put on a benefit dinner this October to raise money for the school?"

Another pause.

"Yes! Let me see what I can do."

I am amazed at her response. There is sweat beading on my forehead. I know Maite is praying for me in the other room.

"I'm sorry to ask you to do such a huge thing. I know this is an enormous task for anyone to do."

"Pastor Roger, God will do this! I know it." Instead of backing away from my request, I can hear her excitement building over the phone. "Let me make a few calls. Don't worry. God can do anything!"

Later she told me she had been in the supermarket deliberating between brands of hot dogs, trying to save a few dollars. But she still manages to help me exhale the anxiety that has been building in my chest in a long, slow breath. Her response is like a fresh breeze blowing away the darkness of the day.

October rolls around. We are in the church fellowship hall. Tables are draped with linens. Candles flicker around the room. Beautiful flower arrangements are at the center of each table. CPC has gone over the top pouring themselves into decorations and preparing for this event.

People mill around, mingling, sipping drinks. Over two hundred are in attendance. There is a sense of excitement in the air. This church has long supported over seventy missionaries, but this is the first time they are putting on a benefit for any one ministry.

Laura and her husband, Mike, cut through the maze of tables to come over to Maite and me. They are a beautiful couple in more ways than one. Their kindness and generosity put us at ease.

Laura grabs our hands. Excitement is etched in her smile and her warm voice. "Can you believe this turnout? I love it!"

We make our way to our table. Pastor Dick Sanner, the missions pastor, graciously opens in prayer, and dinner is served.

The outpouring of love and funds on this night is overwhelming. Over $80,000 is raised for our school in one night.

I put my head in my hands as relief rolls over me in waves. Nothing like this has ever been done for us before. A chain of events is set in motion on this night that will change the course of our lives.

A few months later, Laura opens the front door to her immaculate and spacious home and greets us before inviting us inside. The beautiful home, with its deep blue pool and wide spaces and impeccable decorating, is on the market. Mike has gotten a promotion in his high-powered building firm, and they are moving to Newport Beach. But Laura is on a mission.

"Welcome! Come in; come in! You're right on time!"

Marie France, Clint, and I step inside and breathe in the clean scent of her home. There are hugs all around. Even after spending many evenings planning the benefit banquet here, I am still overwhelmed by the beauty of Laura's home every time I visit.

"Okay, kids, come on. We are going to meet Dad at the church," Laura calls over her shoulder as she fastens on her earrings. Grabbing her fur coat up off of a chair, she turns to us and grins, her blue eyes sparkling. "We're going to get this thing done before I move. I know God can do this. I know when they hear your story they are going to want to help you."

Marie France and Clint are chatting quietly in the car as we drive to the church. I can tell they are nervous like I am. We are meeting with the missions committee at CPC for the first time. We want them to take us on as a project and help us fix the code violations. My stomach is in knots.

Okay, God, please help us.

Mike is there when we get there.

"Thanks, honey, for taking the kids." Laura kisses him good-bye as he bundles the kids off, leaving us to our meeting. Turning to me with a determined look, she says, "Roger, you can do this. Be strong."

My nerves must be showing on my face.

"God has worked this out so far. This is going to be good. I will tie up the loose ends," Laura assures me.

We enter the church and find our way back to the conference room. Some of the people I recognize from the benefit. Laura is completely at ease, laughing and introducing us around the table. The missions pastor gets us started.

"I'd like to introduce Roger Huang, his daughter Marie France, and her husband, Clint. They are with us tonight to tell us about their work in the Tenderloin. Let's welcome them."

There is a polite applause, and then they start the DVD telling about our ministry. Images of the Tenderloin flash on the screen. Faces that I know and love. People who are broken. People whose lives have been changed by getting to know Jesus.

Each ministry is highlighted, from the school to the Homeless Café to the volunteer center. So much is riding on this meeting. My palms are slick with sweat. The DVD comes to an end. A hush settles over the room as they take in the gravity of life in the Tenderloin.

Marie France is the first to speak. "First of all, I want to thank you for all you have already done for us. We were blessed by all you did for us with the banquet, and you should know that we are so thankful."

She is beautiful, my daughter, standing and speaking passionately about the school. I am proud of her in so many ways. Her incredible heart for the ministry. The dreams she carries in her heart about what the school can become. Her skill as an administrator and teacher. Her love for the students. The way she cares for her own children and weaves her home life and ministry together.

Clint stands to join her and talks about the rescue mission and the daily care of the homeless and destitute on our streets. His smile and quick sense of humor engage the room immediately.

I lose myself thinking about them, these kids of ours who have joined us in giving their lives in the Tenderloin. Clint and Marie France decided to stay with us permanently after Clint hurt his knee playing basketball overseas. They had always planned to go back so that Clint could play again. God had other plans.

The way they stepped into the ministry, it was as if they had always been there. It was more than we could hope for. Clint is an incredibly hard worker and is disciplined in the pursuit of excellence, whether it's teaching a child to play basketball or spending time in his personal devotions. Always willing to help in any area, whether it is throwing sports camps or knocking on doors, he is always ready. Clint went from organizing our food bank to becoming program director of the rescue mission. I am constantly amazed by the care and love he shows the people of the Tenderloin.

Laughter brings my attention back to the front of the room.

"And now Roger is going to come and share about the needs we currently have for the building." Clint nods toward me and places a hand on Marie France's back, guiding her toward a chair.

Clearing my throat, I stand in front of this group of men and women and pour out my heart for the Tenderloin, telling story after story of the lives that have been touched at 230 Jones. As I start to close my talk, my mind flashes back to those pictures we had seen earlier. The kids who don't know if they will get a meal. The homeless man who struggles to find his place and make his way in this life. The drug addict who needs one more chance and an encounter with the God who loves him. The needs these people have are so intense I can feel them in my bones.

Tears begin to flood my eyes. My voice cracks.

"If you could just help us, we really need this building to keep ministering, to keep sharing the love of Jesus and feeding people."

My emotion silences me, and I look to see that my tears are mirrored in the faces before me. Everyone is crying. Laura. Marie France. The missions committee.

Without a word, they gather around me to lay hands on me.

A man to my left prays fervently, "God, You know we are looking for a place to serve. We have been talking about a local ministry and here they are. Please confirm in our hearts if this is the one we need to help."

I answer his prayer with a silent prayer of my own. "God, let them know this is the one. There is no need to pray. We are sinking and there is no way out."

We thank everyone and head out to the car.

Laura hugs us all. "I know that God is going to do this. I'm sure of it."

I cling to that hope as I get in the car. I try not to get too excited. I have been disappointed before.

But God is faithful. It is as if He has opened the heavens and poured out His favor on us. CPC is in for the long haul. It is as if years of prayers are culminating in this one moment. And I can hardly believe it.

■ ■ ■

Looking at the interior of 230 Jones, it is unrecognizable. Clods of plaster are everywhere. The back staircase is cordoned off. The staff has moved out of their third-floor lodgings since the last deluge of rain soaked us all. We are in full renovation mode. I am amazed as I see a hundred volunteers carrying buckets of debris, hammering, cleaning, roaming the halls of our building.

"Roger?"

I look up as a gentleman with neat, silver hair strides toward me.

"Fred, how are you doing this morning?"

"I am great. Is there anything I can do for you?"

He takes off his glasses and clears the dust from them. We are all breathing it in. Weekends are when the most volunteers can come and help us.

"Nope, I'm just checking all the floors to see how everything is going. Want to join me?"

We head up the stairs, talking shop about what needs to be done.

"Hey, Dad! Hey, Fred!" Michelle stops us in the hall. She is working on getting volunteers together for our huge Thanksgiving outreach and starts telling Fred about it. Fred laughs. I can see the affection he has for my daughter in his smile. It makes me grateful for this man. This man who changed my life and my ministry.

Pastor Scott Farmer, the lead pastor at CPC, has given us a dream team to push this vision forward. We are overwhelmed on a daily basis by their graciousness. The moment after CPC decided to help us and renovate our building, our path changed course. Help was on its way. Our prayers had been answered.

Fred was one of those answered prayers.

Fred is a renowned builder who has built thousands of houses in the Bay Area along with heading up multiple building teams for missions projects. His expertise in building is beyond me. He lives and breathes it.

But as he began scouting the project for CPC and looking at the building, he was silent. He didn't share about how they were going to fix the violations and get the building up to code. He just kept coming to the building, walking the stairs, viewing the problem areas, making notes to himself.

The morning everything shifted was when Fred looked at me and said, "Roger, you just want us to fix the fire-code violations so you can keep these two classrooms in your school going. But what if we don't just fix the problems? What if we gut this building completely? What if we give you a whole new building with room for three hundred students? How would you feel about that?"

I was stunned. Speechless.

"How?"

"We are going to build you a new building, and we will lay out a ten-year controlled growth plan for you. We will build a school that will fit 350 students, not just thirty. We are going to do this the right way."

An unbelievable joy filled me. This was nothing we prayed for. This was God one-upping us, showing how great and amazing He is, going beyond our wildest dreams and hopes and giving us a place of permanence in the Tenderloin. A place that will be fully functional and beautiful and better than anything I could have imagined.

With my heart full and a smile stretched across my face, I grasped Fred's hand in my own. He was rooting for us. Pulling for God to do good things for us. I didn't really know how to respond to such generosity and support. But I was going with it. All the way.

Fred and Jan Hull give three years of their life to build our four-story school building, all the while tending to their family business in Reno. They are more than just husband and wife. They are part-ners in mission. Their love for each other poured out into love for the poor of the Tenderloin community. They make taking on such a daunting task seem easy and effortless. Fred manages the construc-tion and Jan manages the finances.

I have always felt more comfortable around women. Maybe it is because of the deep scarring I still struggle with from my father's cruelty. But I have found that women will give their lives for something that touches their hearts. Maite likes to say that I run a women's ministry since we have so many women volunteers. So many fantastic women have given their lives, their time, their money, enabling us to do what God has asked us to do, and without them we would be nothing.

But when Fred stepped into my life, something changed. I found a man passionate about the things of God, willing to work hard with me, willing to take responsibility for what God had laid on his heart. When I had meetings with him regarding personal issues, I found him to be a man of love and compassion. I found a man who gave me hope and who gave without reservation. My loner thinking had to shift. For the first time, someone was shouldering this burden with me, which is so heavy, shouldering the weight of souls and needs as well as the changes that had to be made in this building process.

Fred's words are backed up by his actions. He doesn't make empty promises. Fred is on the phones, emailing, calling, gathering volunteers, encouraging, keeping people on task. God has called him to do the impossible by building this building with volunteer labor and to fund it with gifts, and he is obeying. His obedience gives me space to breathe. There is not a day that goes by that I do not thank God for Fred.

Along with Fred, churches all over California joined in funding the renovations. Volunteers poured in every weekend. Individuals gave their all—their money, their sweat, their hearts—in making over our building.

There is not one dry eye in the place three years later when we stand in front of a new 230 Jones—complete, whole, and revitalized in its renovations.

I stand at the door. A crowd fills the streets. The excitement is palpable. My family stands next to me, along with our partner church from Danville. The sun is bright in the sky. It is as though God is beaming down His pleasure upon us.

A prayer of dedication is lifted up. "God, we thank You for this building. For the thousands of hands that built it. For the heart that went into it. Use this building for Your purposes. Amen!"

The cheers are deafening. Whistles, hollers, and hallelujahs fill the streets. The doors of 230 Jones open again into bright white halls, spotless classrooms, wide hallways, and a completely reconfigured ministry center.

And the craziest thing is that the miracles don't stop here. It seems God is on a roll. The renovations of 230 Jones are just the beginning. And the people God is bringing to the Tenderloin to minister alongside of us with compassion and dedication continue to amaze me.

I like to say I am God's bellhop. I just open the doors that He asks me to, and He does all the work. It is a beautiful and crazy life that God has given us in the Tenderloin. And He just keeps surprising us with how He works everything out.

Chapter 19

LIVES CHANGED IN THE TENDERLOIN

Tenderloin, 2010
Hidden treasure.

The smell of fresh paint still lingers in the hallway of 230 Jones. The walls are a crisp white, and I can hear the laughter of children echo off of them as I take the stairs from the third floor, where my prayer room/office is, to the main level. I am getting ready to go around the corner to check out the new medical clinic that Clint has started in the back of the rescue mission on Turk Street.

Who would have thought that this former strip club would one day house a triage center as well as the feeding ministry to the Tenderloin's homeless community? The Homeless Café is set up to feed the bellies and souls of all who walk through its doors. Each meal is preceded by a talk about God's grace and love. Each meal is prepared by the hands of those who have felt God's grace and love walked out in their own lives. Like Kurt.

Three years ago he'd found himself out of a job, homeless, and living in a shelter with his wife. Dreams were at a minimum. Despair was at a maximum. Tucked away in a back corner of the rescue mission, waiting for the meal service to begin, he heard Pastor Clint say, "If you come and volunteer here, God will bless you immensely and do miraculous things in your life."

Kurt figured he had tried everything else and that he would give it a shot. He began volunteering, and three weeks later he was offered a job. He couldn't believe it. He kept volunteering. He was offered two more jobs.

Amazed, he and his wife hoped they could be out of the shelter and find a place by Christmas. A week later, a landlord came by the shelter with news of a place opening up. They were in it a week before Christmas.

Kurt is a changed man. The man who had lost all hope and who had just dropped into the rescue mission looking for his next meal now leads outreach efforts in the Tenderloin, opens up the Café's dinner hour with prayer, and is a part of the discipleship team.

We have seen God begin His work using a warm cup of soup and a piece of bread to soften someone's heart toward the God who chases after us with His love and goodness. Stories like Kurt's fill us with hope and keep us going as we struggle to make an impact in the Tenderloin

I stop by the second floor to check in with Maite and sign a few checks for our ongoing bills.

"Just a few more." She smiles, pushing the checks across the desk to me.

This part of the ministry never stops. There are always needs to be filled. Bills to be paid. Problems to be solved. Maite is my partner in every aspect of this work. Bookkeeping isn't her favorite thing to do, but she steps in and helps wherever she is needed. Pictures of our grandkids crowd her desk. Colorful notes from the students are taped to the wall. She brings love to whatever she does and everyone feels it. I feel her strength behind me and with me at each turn. I want her with me all the time.

I grab her hand and squeeze it across the desk. "I'll be back in a few minutes. Let's grab something to eat."

She nods. "Sounds good."

She is already looking back at her computer, working out the next set of problems. God still amazes me through the woman He gave me. With her laughter, her love, her acceptance of me.

I was telling her the other day, "Maite, this whole ministry thing, it just came out of left field." Two immigrants in America trying to win the world for Jesus.

With a lift of her eyebrow, she said, "Yeah, I know, Roger. The problem is, we are still in left field."

We can only laugh. I'll take left field if it means being with Maite. Her wisdom and strength shore me up daily. Looking back through the years, she has kept me grounded in more ways than one. And she will be the first to tell you that I need it. I tend to agree with her.

Down the hall, in a classroom, I hear a familiar voice. I pop my head in. Beth, one of our volunteers from Community Presbyterian Church, is here to tutor one of our students. Heads bent toward each other, one gray and one brown, they are hard at work. Hearing my footsteps, they turn to look at me. Beth's eyes are twinkling.

"Hi, Pastor Roger! We are really getting this reading thing down!"

The boy ducks his head a little in embarrassment. I put a hand on his shoulder.

"That is great! I love to hear that. Beth, thank you for being here with us."

Beth has been a force to be reckoned with since she stepped through our doors. She is such a part of the daily fabric of our ministry we can no longer imagine what City Academy was like before she arrived. Gathering troops and bringing them with her, she comes each week to tutor. She collects school supplies, socks, and money to donate for the students. Beth is motivated by the great love she has for these children. She prays for them, encourages them, challenges them. She has her own key to lock up, as she goes above and beyond what a normal volunteer does. Last year, she led the charge on food planning and cooking at our Fort Bragg kids camp at the Blessing Home, lifting burden after burden from our shoulders. Beth is invaluable.

"We are so thankful you are here. You know that, don't you?"

Her eyes crinkle at the corners as she smiles and places a hand on the boy's shoulder. "There is no place I would rather be."

In this moment I don't know that Beth's time with us will be far too short. In a little less than a year, cancer will claim her. From her hospital bed, she still gave orders about raising money and providing food for our summer camp.

When we told the students Miss Beth had died, one of them asked, "Is Miss Beth in heaven?"

We said, "Yes."

The student replied, "Then I want to go there too."

Beth left us too soon. Sometimes we think we change the lives of those who come to volunteer with us here in the Tenderloin. But the opposite holds true too. Beth changed us inside and out. Her fingerprints are all over our souls, and her love is ingrained in the hearts of these little ones. They will not soon forget her.

Walking the length of the hall, I take one more flight of steps down, and I am finally on the main floor. I pass the kitchen and look in to see Veasna and a couple of volunteers in the kitchen prepping lunch for the students at City Academy. We have gone from thirty to seventy students since our expansion. Each day, we offer a hot lunch for our students. Warm food in the belly goes a long way toward helping each child learn.

The smell of sizzling onions in the pan wafts out the door. I pop my head in.

"How's it going?"

Veasna looks over his shoulder. His smile lights up his face. It is a great smile. "Good, Pastor Roger. We just got a new shipment in."

"Great!" I smile back at him.

Different grocery stores around the city give us their leftover items. We send our drivers daily to pick up all the donations. The food finds its way into the community through the rescue mission, our food bank, and our outreach teams that make grocery deliveries. The food never goes to waste. It is a physical representation of God's love in this community, of a God who cares about these people and their most basic needs.

Veasna's story with us began when, as a child, he would visit the rescue mission. I remember when he was a little boy and he only came to us to eat and get gifts. I also remember him as a troubled youth, trying to find his way on the streets.

Veasna's family escaped the horrors of the Khmer Rhouge in Cambodia during the 1980s. His mother was pregnant with him when she and his father made their perilous journey, by night, through the sniper-filled jungle toward a refugee camp. It took them weeks to get there.

Once in the refugee camp, many around them died of starvation. Veasna's dad, who was a congressman in Cambodia, managed to get them to San Francisco. But the dreams of a new life were crushed by the realities of trying to build a new life in the Tenderloin. They tried to make it work. But after years of struggle, Veasna's dad left them to return to Cambodia to teach. His mom was left to cope with raising their family on her own.

In despair, Veasna turned to gangs and drugs to escape. Ecstasy and raves were his sanctuary. Different people reached out to him from our center, but he was unmoved. Chasing away the pain of life with drugs and parties was his biggest high. Until one morning, when something shifted in his life.

He found himself at the back of our church, overwhelmed by a sense of peace and euphoria, something better than any high he had ever felt. He didn't know that he had just come in contact with the Holy Spirit. My son Chris, a high schooler at the time, asked him to move into 230 Jones with him so they could pray together. They were the first to live in the building.

The gangster turned into a prayer warrior as God began to change him from the inside out. Veasna has never looked back. He became a youth intern, and all these years later, he stands in our kitchen, a man full of God's grace, a teacher at City Academy.

He pours out his life on a daily basis for these kids, knowing the transforming power of God's love in his own life. He is bringing hope and love to these kids daily. I love him like he is my own son.

Pushing through the front door and past the gate, I glance up the street. I see Teacher Laura with her kindergarteners at Boedekker Park. They stand in a circle playing a game. She is laughing. I can hear the sound of her joy over the idling car engines at the light and the chatter on the sidewalk.

Laura's joy is contagious. But I remember a time when happiness was hard to come by for her. Laura's childhood story is one of heartache.

Laura's family also escaped the horrors of Cambodia. But despite the new start in America, troubles seemed to plague their family. With seven people crammed into a one-bedroom apartment, tempers ran hot. Her dad was both physically and emotionally abusive. He finally left the family when Laura was ten. Her mom died when she was just fifteen, leaving her and her brothers on the streets in the Tenderloin.

Sometimes Laura would find a couch at a friend's house to sleep on. Sometimes she would stay up all night, roaming the streets. She dropped out of high school. Her brothers sold drugs to keep the family fed. These were years of tears and despair. She tried to stay high as much as she could to keep from feeling the pain of her life.

Coming from a Buddhist background, there was still a deep need for God in Laura's life. She began searching for Him. One night, she passed the rescue mission during a Friday-night youth-group meeting. She saw Pastor Chris and asked him for a Bible. She began reading it, not understanding it, but hungry for a truth that would transform her life. She would come to youth meetings and sit in the back, high on marijuana, and listen to the worship songs.

Chris and his future wife, Cori, an intern at the time, kept loving her and visiting her, even bringing her a mixtape of worship songs on her eighteenth birthday. The reality of God's love began to get her in its grip.

At eighteen, Laura went back to continuation school to graduate from high school. Her teacher just happened to be a spirit-filled Christian and would take Laura out into the hall to pray for her. God's love was shoring her up on every side, encompassing her.

Laura joined the internship program at 230 Jones, growing in her faith. Her life is a beacon of love, shining on everyone she is around. Not only does she teach kindergarten, she is our youth pastor. Her heart beats for the Tenderloin and the kids who walk these streets. She has walked in their shoes. She wants to love them into the arms of Jesus like she was.

I call her my adopted daughter. I see the love of God in her eyes when she looks at her students, in her actions when she goes door-to-door handing out groceries, and in the way she lives out her life. It is beautiful to behold, and so is she.

The business of the Tenderloin never stops. The bartering for drugs. The wrangling a living off of these mean streets. There is a sense of hopelessness that swallows the homeless community, but that is why we are here. Jesus came to mend the broken and heal the dying. It makes sense that He has plunked a broken and lost man like myself into a community of broken and lost people. I know the pain of abuse and the loneliness of rejection. I've slept in storefront doorways and endured weeks of stomach-stabbing hunger. I see my former fears and anxieties harbored in the eyes of the lost on these streets. And I am hoping that they see God's love in mine. That they can see someone just like them whom God has lifted out of the pit of life and set on solid ground. He can do the same for them.

Across the street, on the diagonal, I can see Teacher Elaine through the glass doors of City Academy. She is striking even at a distance. She is getting ready to join Laura's class at the park.

When Elaine first came to visit us, she came to donate clothes. She had a good job and income. She was living a successful life, but coming to help us out was her undoing. Not only did she come to volunteer, donating her time, but she felt God asking her to give more. He wanted her to come here to live and serve. She left her job, her stable environment, and came to live at 230 Jones on the third floor. Elaine gave up all she had and knew to follow this new path of being a teacher to children who struggle in so many ways every single day. Coming here changed everything for her. Not only did she fall in love with the Tenderloin, she fell in love with Veasna. Married, they are raising their family here, all while serving with us.

Elaine spends each day ministering to families, engaging them, encouraging them, telling them about Jesus's love. It was not a coincidence that brought her to us. It was the gracious hand of God. She blesses us on a daily basis.

I turn to my left, heading toward the rescue mission. It is another windswept day in the Tenderloin. A full, crazy, busy day. But I am overwhelmed by the richness of the lives that I am surrounded by. Each person I have come in contact with today has shaped me.

Their stories, their hopes, their dreams have collided with mine, and together, we are making a difference. Each on our own journeys, imperfect, constantly changing, we are working together to bring light into the darkness of these San Francisco streets. We long for the transformation of others as we have been transformed. We hope for God's grace and mercy to flood these buildings with hope, shutting out the despair that so frequently fills the derelict halls and these desperate lives. And together, we pray. For more workers. More volunteers. More helpers to bring their talents and hearts with them here to San Francisco. God is still at work changing lives. Moment by moment. Hour by hour. And He never ceases to amaze us with the people He brings to help us. His timing is impeccable.

Chapter 20

PRAYING AND FASTING
FOR WORKERS

Tenderloin, 2010
God is love. He loves everyone.

Nothing ever comes easy in the Tenderloin. It is just the way it is. We fast. We pray. We wait on God. And in His timing, in His graciousness, He moves on our behalf.

I have learned, over the years, that fasting is the way I connect with God and let Him know how serious I am. Driven by desperation of the situation, I call out to Him and He always responds. He knows our needs. He knows our hearts.

We are on our way to the Blessing Home. A cool wind blows in off the coast as we make our way up the wooded hill toward the house. Renovations have been coming along on the house. A new roof. New windows. New flooring. We work as hard as we can, and God sends people to help us. Each time God brings someone, or a team of individuals, with a talent or a skill, it takes us one step closer to where we need to be.

We are going up to pray about the ministry. The six-thousand-square-foot home still amazes us when we step inside. The vaulted ceilings and wide windows offer a spectacular view of the sprawling ocean as we look down the hill and past Highway 1.

A white board stands in the corner of the room where we serve breakfast for our summer camp. The needs from our last prayer time here stretch across the board in a blue scrawl. I rub them away with my hand and pick up the white-board pen, adding the new requests.

I turn to Maite. Her profile is caught in a blaze of pale oranges and yellows as the afternoon sun sets through the window.

"Okay, Maite. You should know that when I pray today, I am planning on going really deep. Really deep. I'm not going to be talking, just praying. We really need to concentrate and ask God to answer these requests."

She nods. "Okay."

She gets me. She understands how I pray and my need for silence when I meditate and wait on the Lord.

We spread a couple of woven mats on the floor. The fading colors of the autumn sun fill the room. I lie facedown on the mat. Focusing. Thinking. Talking to God. I find that it's best to just bring one or two things to Him at a time. He knows my heart. He needs to know I am willing to wait on Him.

I press in. The next thing I know the room is dark and the sun is hiding behind a bank of clouds. I sit up, realizing I fell asleep. Maite is sitting cross-legged on her mat. Her arms are folded across her chest. She is not praying. She has a smirk on her face.

"Going deep, huh? You went real deep. You were so deep, you were snoring."

Laughing, I say, "That's pretty deep."

She laughs with me. Sometimes prayer and laughter go hand in hand. Or prayer and sleeping for that matter.

"Maite, let's pray for Chris. Again."

Maite grabs my hand. This time we pray together. Our hearts are joined in this.

Chris and his wife, Cori, left the Tenderloin a few years ago to work at a different church. He is now working for a company in Modesto near Cori's family. Cori's dad, Ben, is one of my closest friends, a renegade for Jesus. On more than one occasion his belief in us and his financial support have turned the tide for us. I love the Hardister family like they are my own. I am thankful the kids are close to the Hardisters, but the fact that Chris is far from us, not working in the ministry, away from the Tenderloin, wrenches me open. It is our greatest dream for all of our kids to work with us. When Chris left, he left a gaping hole in our hearts.

I have always tried to be a good dad. I never had anyone to show me how to do that. I have always struggled, carrying the scars of my past into each relationship I have. I have done the best I know how. But I know that Chris was hurt when he left. I know that he wanted more from me. I didn't do everything right. But then, no parent does. We are all broken in some way.

Once again I find myself battling old demons. Rejection. Hopelessness. A fear that the family relationship I long for isn't possible. That I have driven Chris away when all I long for is for him to be with us.

I close my eyes and breathe in deeply, letting some of the stress escape as I exhale. Maybe it is a selfish way to pray. That God will bring my family close and they will have a passion to serve with us. But I have seen Him answer this prayer with my other children.

When Marie France and Clint decided to stay with us, it shifted our entire ministry. Suddenly, these two were shouldering burdens with us. And it wasn't just our burden; God gave each of them a heart, a passion that was all their own. Watching that happen seemed like a miracle. It was a miracle.

Maite and I lean toward each other. The dark shadows of the pine trees around the house dim the room.

"God, we are asking You to bring Christian back to us. To bring Cori and the kids. We don't know how You will do it. We don't know how You will change their hearts or bring the finances so that they can come, but we leave it with You. We know You can do it. You have done it before."

The wind whistles through the branches outside.

We know He can change hearts. He led Michelle back to us.

Michelle had left college and was doing temp work in the city. She wanted to spread her wings. To live life away from Mom and Dad. Most kids do. But I knew she didn't love her work, that it was just a way to make ends meet. I met her one day for lunch. Her long black hair framed her face. Her smile lit her entire face. I love her face. This girl gives me joy.

"Michelle, how much do you need to live on? How much are they paying you at the temp agency?"

She stirs the water in her glass with her straw. "I don't know, Dad—"

I cut her off. "Michelle, we want you to come work with us. We can pay you more than they do at the temp agency. We need you. We need your help."

It only takes her moments to decide. "Okay, Dad, I'll do it."

My heart is full. Overfull. The thought of being around her every day lifts me.

She begins by helping in the office. Filing. Helping with bills. In weeks, Michelle has turned our volunteer department around, putting a system in place for the teams that come from churches to help us regularly. In a year, she has transformed it, bringing order to the chaos. Organizing the huge community outreaches that we put on during the holidays, she continues to shape the process, making it easier for volunteers to sign up and be used to help minister to the poor, to encourage those who live in our community.

Maite and I are continually amazed by the young woman she has become. She is no-nonsense, funny, easy to work with, and welcoming. Michelle brings her love of life, her laughter, to everything she does. Even her wedding was a spectacle of joy. Done in true Michelle style. My mind drifts back to the bright day in August a few months earlier.

The corner of Jones and Eddy was cordoned off. Down the center of the street was a middle aisle framed by rows of white folding chairs. The sound of traffic was muted as it followed the detour past our street. The sky was blue, shaking off its normal fog. And the music was swelling, filling the streets.

Receiving special permission from the city council, Michelle and her fiancé, Jody, had chosen to be married in front of City Impact in the middle of Jones Street. I looked at her as we stood shoulder to shoulder. This beautiful daughter of mine. She never does anything halfway.

Her long hair lifted off her shoulders in the breeze as we started down the aisle. She had my heart. She always has. I followed her gaze to her groom. A musician who had won her heart, Jody was smiling, mirroring Michelle's happiness. She was looking toward her future.

Friends and family looked back, watching us as we made our way up the aisle. I couldn't help smiling. A sense of excitement rippled up the rows as we passed. Only Michelle would have her wedding in the middle of the Tenderloin. But feeling the moment and its impact, it was unique, breathtaking, and inspiring, like she is.

I am so thankful that God brought her back to us.

God continually amazes us with the people He brings to bless us. He has brought us people we wouldn't dream of needing to pray for.

Earlier in the year, as the renovations were being completed, I was in the car with Maite. Driving toward the car park, I spotted an elegant lady with two equally elegant friends standing in front of our building. Squinting, I recognized Eli, a friend and donor from the Bay Area.

"Maite, that's Eli! Let me jump out here."

Running across the street, I thrust my hand out in front of me. "Eli! How are you? What are you doing here?"

Her face lit with recognition. "Pastor Roger, I've brought a couple of my closest friends with me. Meet Kristin and Leslie. I had to bring them up here to see what's going on."

Smiling, I shook hands with them. Kristin and Leslie are both tall, blonde, and striking in their features.

"Eli has been telling us about the work you are doing here. We had to come see for ourselves." Kristin grinned.

Eli and her husband, David, have been crucial partners in our financial support. An influential businessman in the video-game industry, David reached out to us, and we have been blessed by them countless times.

Just this past year, they threw a fund-raiser for us with their friends. When only two guests RSVP'd, Eli thought we should cancel. I told her, "Let's go with it. You never know what could happen."

We ended up having an amazing evening. That was the night we were introduced to Ted and Sarah, a stunning couple who are close friends of Eli and David's. They were moved by what we were doing in the Tenderloin and wanted to get involved. Ted, a director in venture capital and assets management, went on to raise a substantial amount for the school. We were amazed.

While over two hundred had been invited to attend the event, God knew we only needed to connect with these two special people. They are now a pivotal part of City Academy, and their generosity has helped us in furthering the development of our classrooms and funding for our students.

We never know how God is going to move or whom He is going to use. We just know He does it better than we could ever imagine. And it seems that God keeps using Eli to introduce us to people who have a heart for the poor.

Opening the door to 230 Jones, the trio stepped inside. I led the three ladies on a full tour. Renovations were still under way, but each room was like a fresh, bright canvas waiting to be completed. I could feel the ladies' excitement building as I showed them the new classrooms, the offices, the renovated kitchen.

"This is amazing!" exclaimed Eli.

Sharing the story of how we came to the Tenderloin and got the building and how Community Presbyterian Church came to renovate it only fueled their excitement. I had no idea what was going on in their minds, but I knew that God was moving them.

Fast-forward three months and Kristin and Leslie have rallied their own troops at their home church of Menlo Park Presbyterian. In a whirlwind of activity, they pick up where CPC left off, outfitting the classrooms with computers that the teachers can use as teaching tools. They bring in funding and stock an entire brand-new, functional library for our kids at City Academy.

One of Leslie's friends, a Bay Area restaurateur, donates a brand-new commercial kitchen, complete with walk-in fridge and freezer. This revolutionizes our entire food output process. We have come a long way from the rice cooker I used to plug in during our first Bible studies back at our building on Eddy.

Kristin and Leslie brought in over nine hundred people in less than two years and gave us beautiful after-school classrooms. Both of them are passionate and selfless, and they always find ways to give to the poor.

Blown away by their leadership and generosity, we are even more stunned when they begin to dream with us, hope with us, and pray with us that God would keep bringing more and more workers to impact this city for Him. We can never outdo the dreams God puts on our hearts.

Since that time, Kristin and Leslie have organized an all-church event, bringing over four hundred MPCC members into the heart of

San Francisco to do everything from delivering meals to organizing our food bank to setting up a tent for free haircuts. Their stamina and excitement over what God is doing are contagious. It won't be long before all of Menlo Park is coming with them.

The sun has set and the night stretches out before us. The smell of freshly brewed coffee wafts from the kitchen. Maite is making us each a cup to warm us up. The chill of the night air is creeping in. The wind picks up off of the coast and has the tree branches rattling against the windows.

Standing at the window in the spacious front room, I look out across the inky sky. God is good. He has proven Himself to us over and over.

Maite stands next to me, handing me a steaming mug of coffee. Her head is on my shoulder.

"We'll just keep praying."

"Going deep," she answers.

Our laughter fills the arced ceiling.

We don't know how or when He will answer our prayers. But we know one thing. He will answer. Answers will come in His timing. In His way. And just like a hundred times before, He completely floors us when He answers our prayer for more workers. In a way that we could never imagine. Not in a million years.

Chapter 21

PRAYING AND FASTING
FOR A CONFERENCE

The Tenderloin, 2011
Men after His own heart.

Sitting on the edge of the bed, I breathe. Slowly. The sounds of foghorns from the bay are muted through my bedroom window. Most people are not yet awake at this early hour, but I find that I think better in the darkness before dawn.

We have four days. Four days before our conference at Parc 55. The irony isn't lost on me, that the first conference we are holding in the Tenderloin is being held at the hotel that brought me to its streets. There is a sort of joy knowing that God has brought us full circle in this way. I left my auditing jobs at both Parc 55 and the Marriott to minister full-time in the Tenderloin. Now we are gathering five hundred people in Parc 55's nicest ballroom to send them out to minister there as well. I wonder if Parc 55 knows it was a launching pad for inner-city ministry.

Running my fingers through my hair, I stand up to walk the room. Maite is still sleeping; her breathing is even and calm.

There is just the small problem of food. We don't have any.

Delivering hot meals and bags of groceries to the residents in our community is one of the most profound ways we share the love of Jesus in our center. It is hard to talk about God's love and faithfulness when the one you are talking to can't hear over the growling of their hungry belly. A loaf of bread and a can of soup can have immense effect on softening the scarred hearts of those who need to hear about Jesus.

One time when Teacher Laura was delivering groceries, the lady she gave them to burst into tears. Laura asked her why she was crying. Opening the bag for Laura to see, she said, "How did you know it was my son's birthday today?" Tucked into the corner of the bag were a birthday cake mix and a container of icing.

"I didn't," Laura said.

But obviously God did.

The God we are chasing after loves us so much He provides cake mix for birthday celebrations.

This is not a regular conference. We are not having breakout sessions. We are sending the attendees out with food to go into the buildings and bless the community. Besides having food for the conference participants, we want to deliver six thousand hot meals and two thousand bags of groceries during the conference. I know that God will provide food for our conference. He has met our needs for each outreach we have done. I don't really worry about things like that anymore. At least not until it is four days before the conference. Then I begin to pray a little harder.

Pacing the floor, I pray. A thought slips into my prayers. *Use your ministry account money to buy chicken drumsticks.*

I have prayed long enough to recognize thoughts that are from the Holy Spirit. I have the distinct sense that we need to step out and spend what we have in the account toward providing for this conference. I rub my forehead and exhale.

Grabbing my clothes and tennis shoes from the closet, I head out for a morning prayer walk along the trails in Golden Gate Park. Maybe God will give me clearer instructions as I walk and pray.

Maite is up and getting ready when I get back to the house. The smell of toast and freshly brewed coffee fills the kitchen. I let her in on the thoughts that have been brewing in my head.

"I'm not sure how this is going to work out, but this is what I feel like God wants me to do."

She nods in agreement. "Let's do it."

I pick up my cell phone and dial. The phone rings. Chris answers the phone.

"Chris?"

"Hey, Dad!" His voice comes clear across the line.

"We are going to use the ministry account to buy chicken legs for the hot meals. It should get us about three thousand drumsticks. I know we need six thousand, but I feel like God wants us to step out in this."

Chris doesn't miss a beat. "Okay, I'm on it."

"Great. I'll see you in a few."

I am not so worried about chicken legs at this point, because I know that God is in the business of doing miracles. What we have prayed for so long has already happened. Chris has come back to San Francisco. This conference was his idea. We are working on it together.

Maite and I have missed Chris like crazy during the past four years. It was a sad day for us when he left. We felt incomplete with him gone and missed Cori and holding our grandkids. We missed the joy and passion that Chris brought to our work and to our lives, the easy laughter that filled the room whenever he teased Maite. I missed our father/son times when we would pray and fast and cry together. Chris's joy for life and love for God touched everyone around him. We felt his place was with us in the Tenderloin, but that was a miracle only God could bring about.

Chris would be the first to admit that he thought he would never come back to San Francisco. Working for a health insurance company in Modesto, he was on his way to the top. Favor seemed to follow him and his boss kept promoting him. He and Cori were well provided for. They were close to family and had great friends there.

But Chris started to have dreams about the Tenderloin. He knew that God was calling him back, giving him a new heart and vision for the work. It was nothing I had said or done; it was God directing Chris in a real and powerful way. I thank God for His faithfulness. He heard our cries and granted our wish.

It was a bright day when I got the email that told me what God had laid on Chris's heart to do. Tears of joy streamed down my face.

"Maite, come read this."

Maite looked at me with concern and then leaned over my computer to read the open letter. I watched the joy break over her like it had me. Chris was coming back.

We were still trying to work out the logistics of Chris moving back. Rents are much higher in San Francisco than in the San Joaquin Valley. The cost of living is extreme. He was still living in Modesto, and we called back and forth.

One morning I got a call from Chris. "Dad, Francis Chan just moved to San Francisco. I think we should get in touch with him. We need to have him come over so we can pray for him."

"Okay… sure." I paused for a moment. "Chris?"

"Yeah, Dad?"

"Who is Francis Chan?"

An audible groan escaped from him. "Come on, Dad. You're kidding, right? Francis is a really well-known author and pastor. His book *Crazy Love* is amazing."

Clearly, Chris knew who he was. If he was important to Chris, he was important to me.

"Okay, let's invite him over."

Chris emailed Francis, welcoming him to San Francisco and inviting him to come see our work. Francis graciously accepted. When I finally met Francis, I was struck by his humble demeanor.

Smiling, he held out his hand in a greeting. He didn't come across as a big author or pastor. He came across as a genuine friend, a man with a huge heart for the things of God. Someone who was kind and funny. His brother, Paul, came with him, and Chris drove over from Modesto to meet with him. They fell into conversation.

Sitting in my office, I was caught by their laughter as they traded ministry stories. They seemed to slide into an easy friendship.

Out of this meeting, an idea began to formulate. Chris had been dreaming of having a conference in the Tenderloin. Not just any conference, but one where the attendees practice what they have been taught, after the speaker talks. People wouldn't just be getting fed. They would walk out their faith and the love of Christ by ministering to the community.

The idea resonated with me and with our heart for this community. Chris moved forward with the idea.

One day, I got an excited call from him. "Dad, I talked to Francis. He has agreed to be the speaker." I could hear the smile in his voice.

"Chris, that is great! I can't believe it!"

And I couldn't help thinking God has an amazing way of working things out. God not only gave me my son back, but by no small miracle, one of the foremost speakers and pastors of our day had seen something in our work that he wanted to be a part of. I shook my head as I set the phone down.

Things rarely go off without a hitch for our outreaches. We often don't see things come together until the last minute.

Trying to organize a conference in the heart of San Francisco for five hundred people isn't easy. Especially when you live in Modesto.

A while ago, I sat across the table from Chris at our favorite Thai restaurant, and I looked at my son. He had grown into an amazing man. He lit up any room with his laughter. He was a leader through and through. But I could see the struggle in him. How do you quit your job, your safety net, uproot your wife and family, and move to a place of uncertainty? I had been there myself. I knew the anxiety of the decision. Leaving the safety of a good-paying job and stepping out into the unknown is enough to make anyone stop and think twice.

"Chris, you can't lead a conference for San Francisco from Modesto. There is no credibility there. You have to be here. Francis needs you to be here, planning it. You have to quit your job and move here if you want this to work."

The waitress topped off our water glasses. The chatter of the other people in the restaurant hummed around us.

Chris was pensive, thinking, his hands folded in front of him. "I know, Dad. I know."

"Let's think this through."

Together, we mapped out a plan for how he could quit his job. All the while, I prayed in the back of my mind, *God, show us how to do this. Give us the finances Chris needs to come on board with us. We don't want to miss out on this opportunity. How are we going to pay him?*

I kept my concerns to myself. Maite and I knew that God would come through. He had to.

Pulling up to the parking garage, a million thoughts are going through my mind. The attendant takes my keys.

"Thanks so much!"

He smiles at me. "Of course, Pastor Roger."

I can feel the hum of activity as I enter 230 Jones. Plunking myself down with a steaming cup of coffee at my desk, I carefully go through the items on my daily checklist and pray over them, that God would help me get through them. Sometimes the checklist can be difficult to fulfill.

I thank God daily for what He has done and the ongoing miracles that take place throughout each day. I am overwhelmed by His grace, His kindness, His miracles, and His provision. Especially in the last few months.

"God, you know I can't thank You enough for getting Chris and Cori here. For making a way for their house to be rented and for them to find a place down the street from us. Thank You for providing the support for them for the entire next year. You constantly amaze me with how You work things out.

"Thank You for sending Francis to us. For this conference. For the fact that over five hundred people have signed up. We can't believe all that You have done. I know that You will find a way for us to get the food that we need to feed everyone. You are always so good to us."

Taking a sip of my coffee, I allow my thoughts to stay in that place of thankfulness, reminding myself that He always comes through for us, every single time.

Pastor Ralph sticks his head in the door. "Pastor Roger?"

"What's up?"

He is grinning from ear to ear. Pastor Ralph is managing the food bank for us.

"You aren't going to believe this, but TJs just called. One of their megafreezers just broke. They said to come and get the food and to bring a truck. A big one!"

A smile breaks across my face. God has done it again.

Popping up from my desk, I walk downstairs to Maite and Chris. "You guys aren't going to believe this. We don't need the chicken legs anymore. God has provided again. This is going to be good." I fill them in on the details.

That night, Maite and I stand in our giant commercial kitchen, which is full of food. Hundreds of thousands of dollars' worth of food and produce. Our freezers are stocked to the ceilings with frozen meat. It took six round trips with a U-Haul truck to get everything transferred.

Our staff—Mike, Brian, Ralph, and Jimmy—spent the entire day loading and unloading all the food. Manna from heaven in the middle of San Francisco.

God didn't stop there. The excitement of this miracle washes over the entire week.

The conference is a huge success. Each person who comes, serves. Each person leaves with the perspective of what it looks like to walk out their faith in a real and loving way amidst the community in the Tenderloin.

And Francis has become a part of us. He comes to City Impact and works with us. He and Chris launch the Adopt-a-Building program on the heels of the conference. Training up workers to take on one building in the Tenderloin at a time, to transform it with the love of God. Not only are the physical needs in the buildings being met, but slowly, the lives of the tenants are being transformed. One person at a time. As one person comes to know Christ in a building, they, in turn, move toward leading someone else to Christ. Faith upon faith. Hope upon hope.

The ministry is constantly shifting and growing.

Leading a group of pastors who have come to visit our center on a tour, I can hear Chris and Francis laughing down the hall. They are planning their next move.

In between his speaking engagements, Francis is here. He talks to the homeless. Passes out food, and visits the poor. He shies away from people wanting to see him because of his celebrity. He is focused on spending his time meeting the needs of poor and broken souls without asking or expecting anything in return.

In this past year, he has invited us to be a part of his life. His family has grown near to my heart. Seeing how they serve the community humbles me. I have not seen someone in his capacity give and serve and commit himself to the poor with such passion and love. He wants nothing more than to please God and fulfill the task given him. Reaching one life at a time.

Francis is another one who has lifted a burden from my shoulders, sharing the work that we do here.

I look at my checklist for the day, and it is almost completed. I will do the rest tomorrow. The years have taught me that everything is urgent, but not everything can be done in a day. It is time to go home.

I go and find Maite. As we head out of the building I glance over the rooms, the floors, the buildings and streets, and I am in awe of what God has done. His faithfulness and His love for souls.

The fog is rolling in. I don't know what tomorrow holds, but I know this: God is still working in the Tenderloin. Moving in the hearts of men and women. Making a way where there is no way.

And I am grateful. Grateful for a son who has returned. Grateful for a new friend who is working with us, encouraging us. Grateful that after all these long years, God is still changing lives and doing miracles in this community. And I am mostly grateful that He keeps letting me be part of it.

Chapter 22

A NEW VISION FOR THE TENDERLOIN

San Francisco, 2012
I will always love you.

The air is cold and crisp. The late-afternoon sun barely peeks through the fog that is beginning to roll in. I pop in to see Michelle and leave her office laughing. Not a day goes by that I am not thankful for the family God has given me.

Maite is somewhere in the building. She is like a mother hen making sure all her chicks are all right. She helps me with day-to-day operations. Talking to people, helping them to understand the genesis of the ministry, defending me when people don't seem to understand me. I have told God I want to go to heaven before she does. I know this is selfish, but I can't imagine my life without her. We will be meeting to pray together soon.

We are at the start of a ten-day fast. Coffee and water get us through the days of prayer. A nearby sex club has decided to hold a party on Easter Sunday. It is time for them to go. I feel it in my spirit. I know that change comes slowly here, but we keep praying for it and believing it will come. The God I am chasing is powerful and creative and has bigger plans for the people of the Tenderloin than sex clubs and drug addiction. Just look at His plans for me.

I think about where I started this journey. Abused and lonely. Rejected and soul sick. Chasing after security and success to shore up the pain that bled out onto anyone I came into contact with.

And I look at where I am now on my journey. On a path to wholeness. To forgiveness and mercy and healing. Chasing after a God who loves me and who has given me a passion for people instead of money. It is still a journey. I am not finished. But I am a whole lot closer than I was when I started. That sad boy from Taipei, ruined from the inside out by fear and loneliness, has become a man buoyed by grace, still imperfect, but finding his place in this city in the wide ocean of God's love.

Maite is coming toward me down the hall, her face framed by that curly brown hair that first caught my attention.

"Are you ready? People will start coming soon."

I stand and zip up my heavy coat. "Yep. I want to pray around the block before we head up there. I'll be back in a few minutes."

We are going up to the roof to prep for our prayer meeting tonight. We are taking a physical stand to ask God for a spiritual victory. Our hearts' desire is to see lives changed by the power of God. Plain and simple. We have been praying for a long time that God would set the people of the Tenderloin free. Each year, we see the workers coming in by the thousands to this great harvest field. God is continually sending in supporters, pastors, and business folk to help us along.

I think back to twenty-eight years ago when it was Maite and me and the kids going door-to-door, praying for people, offering hope with one hand and a bologna sandwich with the other.

Now, each Thanksgiving and Christmas, over twenty thousand meals and ten thousand grocery bags are distributed to the apartment buildings in the Tenderloin. It is unreal. In my wildest dreams, I couldn't imagine the journey that God has taken us on.

From Taipei to San Francisco, from Parc 55 to the Cadillac Hotel, from darkness to light, from a life of seeking success in order to feel safe to a life of serving others in order to become whole. From a childhood full of horror and rejection to a marriage to a French Basque girl who has loved me through my weakness and pain and taught me how to love her back. From a heart stuck in a place full of bitterness and hatred toward my parents to a heart that seeks to forgive and move forward in God's grace and mercy. I am far from perfect, but still God has loved me, working in and through me. And He has given me a passion to share that love with the ones who remind me of myself. The broken and dispirited. The worn-out and forgotten. The beaten down and unloved. These are my people. I would do anything for them.

FAQS ABOUT PRAYER AND FASTING

What is the reason for fasting?

I fast when I need help and there is no one but God who can help me. When there is a situation that is out of control in the physical world, fasting is an act of desperation as well as an act of supplication to a powerful and living God.

What things have you fasted for in your life?

I fasted when I asked God to expand my family. I fast to keep my marriage pure. I fasted to ask God to heal my brokenness. I fast to ask God's direction, to ask Him to give me a purpose in life and that He will keep me on course.

Why did you start fasting?

When I started following Jesus, I was tired of living from day to day without a purpose. I wanted more than a regular job and the routine of going to church. Bible studies, men's retreats, and worship services weren't enough for me. I wanted to see results in my life, and I wanted to see changes that I could not bring about on my own. I wanted something different. I wanted to be consumed by God's plan for me. I needed God to give me peace and fulfillment.

How do you determine how long you will fast?

The number of days I fast depends on the urgency of the matter. I often follow the number of days that are mentioned in the Bible: one day, three days, seven days, twenty-one days, or forty days. I keep fasting until I see results. For example, I will fast for three days about an urgent matter. I then wait a week, and if I sense the pressure of that situation is still there, I will fast another three days. I will deal with the same issue until it is resolved. The more serious the issue is, the longer I fast.

Of all the personal issues for which I have fasted, I think quitting smoking was the hardest for me. It took three years until the power of that addiction over me was broken. But I kept fasting until the desire for it was taken away from me. I had to quit smoking because it stopped me from praying for more than twenty minutes at a time. Once I quit smoking I was able to pray for hours and days.

How frequently do you fast?

I fast as many times as I need to, and I fast till I get somewhere. I usually fast about one issue at a time. I don't skip and hop around on several urgent issues. I focus on one need at a time. I don't spend a lot of time trying to pace myself or understand the right and wrong way to fast. I just stop eating and present the issue to God.

Who should fast?

Anyone who is desperate should fast. Anyone who is willing and who wants more meaningful guidance from the living God can fast and hear from Him.

What is the temptation during fasting?

There are a lot of temptations while you are fasting. Hunger, distractions from the outside world, and personal needs and desires are usually strongest in the beginning part of fasting. Then it shifts to weariness and lack of concentration. Finally, depression can set in, when it may seem like no one cares about you and you are all alone in this insignificant encounter. Just remember to read the Bible, listen to worship songs, pray, and get quiet within yourself to encourage and build yourself up.

Where do you fast?

I like removing myself from daily life to fast. A remote or isolated place is good. I turn off all the digital devices so I can concentrate on what I am praying about. I love to go to the coast and fast at a cabin or go to a spot that is totally surrounded by nature. It puts me in the right frame of mind for my fasting and prayer time.

What do you bring when you fast?

When I go away to fast, I bring water, juice, and coffee. I also take my Bible, a dictionary (not a smartphone), a notebook, a sleeping bag, and an electric lamp. I take anything that will make me comfortable. I want to ensure I stay warm. When I get too cold, it can be distracting. I love to get a mat, a thick sleeping bag, and a thick jacket. If I don't, I usually get cold and sleepy and that makes it hard to pray.

What do you do while you are fasting?

I use this time alone with God to meditate, read, sleep, walk around, think, talk, wait, listen, and rest. I don't usually feel anything or focus on God till the second or third day due to the thoughts in my mind and the issues that I am carrying with me from the week before. I begin to purge them out of my system by giving them to God or trying to close off my mind and slowly shifting my thinking to my relationship with God. The intimacy with Him usually starts on the second or third day. It's hard to jump into a time of fasting and pretend everything is okay right away. I need to prepare myself and cleanse everything that might hinder my spiritual communication.

What do you ask God for when you pray?

I ask God what He wants to do in me first. I ask myself what I feel is the most important thing in my life right now. It's important to remember that my relationship with God comes first before asking Him for anything.

I ask God to take away the burden of my family issues, to help my marriage, to heal my relationships with others, and to help me overcome my personal struggles, such as my lack of confidence and my lack of knowledge in how to complete a certain task. I don't usually ask for money or material things, but I do ask God to help me with what I need. I don't wish to seek God for personal gain. Fasting is not a lottery system.

I spend a lot of time asking God to heal me and help me love my wife. I know if I am not right with her, then my prayers will be hindered.

I then shift my attention to anyone who is causing problems for me and making my life difficult. I ask God to keep them away from me and move them to another place. Most of my grievances come from difficult people, so I pay attention to asking God to move them so that I can have peace. Life is short.

When do you see the results of your fast?

Most of the time I see results by sticking around and waiting on God. The results may not come while I am fasting, but afterward I gradually see the results of what I have been praying for.

I don't list off the things I want. I take one thing at a time. God is not a businessman. He is a personal friend who knows what I need and when I need it. He has given me everything I asked for and everything I have ever needed. Money is the last thing I have ever needed to concentrate on.

I don't ever set a specific time for God to act upon my plea. I just pray and fast and then know in my heart that it is going to be resolved.

Just know that whatever burden you have in your heart is the very thing that God wants you to pray for. If you want to love a person but it's been difficult to do that, then it's God who wants you to make that relationship right. If you feel the need to give something to someone, then that is the very thing God wants you to do.

I live for that inner voice, that moment of clarity and divine opportunity. I have struggled at times to go against it, but over time, it gets easier and easier to say yes to what God is asking me to do.

Who benefits when you fast?

I do. The person who is fasting always benefits from the fast. If I am obedient to God, then He will continue to answer me and call me into action. Prayer and fasting will change you, but you must act upon it. A good Christian stays in one spot. A great Christian moves forward with obedience. Serving God is not about feelings or emotions. Believe me. It is hard but rewarding.

What is the difference between prayer and supplication?

The intensity. The difference between prayer and supplication is the difference between a gradual prayer and an outcry. I pray often about things I want to see changed. I cry often when I know it has to change.

In one case, I was praying and fasting about my inner struggle with my daughter. I couldn't seem to understand her, but I wanted to do what was right. I wanted to love her without any expectations. That was what I needed to do, but my flesh was in the way. I would travail and wait on God for days and weeks, because I needed God to intervene. My focus was on God and the subject at hand. I would get up in the morning to walk around the block at 3:00 or 4:00 a.m. and pray for God to change me. I would do that day after day in the early morning and eventually I felt the change.

It is hard to change. I don't always like what I ask of God, but I know it is the right thing to do. The experience of prayer and fasting has made me a better person. I am more in tune with God because of it.